TEACH YOUR CHILD TO SWIM

AN INSTRUCTIONAL GUIDE TO THE BASICS OF SWIMMING

Eva Bory

Photographs by Vali Garay

A FIRESIDE BOOK
PUBLISHED BY SIMON & SCHUSTER
New York • London • Tokyo • Sydney • Toronto • Singapore

FIRESIDE
Simon & Schuster Building
Rockefeller Center
1230 Avenue of the Americas
New York, New York 10020

FIRESIDE and colophon are registered trademarks
of Simon & Schuster Inc.

Designed by Stanley S. Drate/Folio Graphics Co. Inc.
Manufactured in the United States of America

10 9 8 7 6 5 4 3 2 1

Library of Congress Cataloging-in-Publication Data

Bory, Eva.
    Teach your child to swim: an instructional guide to the basics of
swimming/Eva Bory.
        p.   cm.
    "A Fireside book."
    1. Swimming for children—Study and teaching. I. Title.
GV837.2.B59   1993
797.2'1'07—dc20   93-3062
                                                                CIP

ISBN 0-671-76995-2

With all my love to Leveleki Eszter, who taught me everything. To Anyu, Bobbie, and also to my only pupil who still can't swim in deep water, Herb.

CKNOWLEDGMENTS

I would like to thank the parents of the children whose photographs were taken for use in this book.

Also a big thanks to my past and future pupils for allowing me to enjoy my work so much.

ONTENTS

PREFACE by Forbes Carlile, M.B.E.M.Sc.   11

1 Some General Thoughts and Advice   15

2 Super Babies (Four Months to Walking Age)   36

3 Walking Age to Three Years   53

4 Three- to Five-Year-Olds   69

5 Five- to Ten-Year-Olds—Advanced Swimming   98

6 Competitive Swimming: Teaching the Butterfly, the Backstroke, the Breaststroke, and the Freestyle   117

INDEX   139

PREFACE

Eva Bory, Hungarian Olympic swimmer and world-record holder, has developed an approach to teaching swimming that is down-to-earth and really works. This is a unique and practical instruction manual, and an individual approach.

This book is no "scissors and paste" job, filled with the half-baked systems of others. It is an original work with ideas well tested both with Eva's daughter and thousands of other children in Australia and America.

Eva Bory, a talented and enthusiastic teacher, is to be congratulated on producing an important exposition of teaching beginning swimming. And she also shows a rare sense of humor, which comes bubbling through in her newly acquired language.

If you have young children or are in the position to help others with their swimming, then this is the book for you.

—FORBES CARLILE, M.B.E.M.Sc.
Former National Coach
Member, International Swimming Hall of Fame
Carlile Swimming Organization, Sydney, Australia

TEACH
YOUR CHILD
TO

1 SOME GENERAL THOUGHTS AND ADVICE

TEACHING THE EASY WAY

There are a few books and pamphlets available on the topic of swimming instruction, most dealing with the subject by giving lesson-by-lesson instructions. The unsuspecting reader gets the impression that it's so easy, just take ten lessons and you are ready for the Olympics! In the first lesson, you learn how to float; in the second lesson, you learn how to kick (the generous ones might throw in arm movements as well); in the third, you learn how to breathe; and so on. But it takes at least ten lessons to teach a three-year-old just to float facedown! This is why I do not deal with lesson progress, but instead explain how to get a child swimming step by step rather than lesson by lesson.

My teaching method consists of dividing swimming into phases or very simple movements, and then, after the baby or child has mastered them one at a time, putting these phases or stages into one more complex movement. Because the rate of learning differs from person to person, you might have to spend ages trying to teach a very simple thing to one child while another will pick it up immediately. Be patient! And kind! My method allows for this individually tailored approach.

START WITH THE BATHTUB

The best way of preparing a child to swim in a swimming pool is to start with a thorough preparation in the bathroom.

Newborn babies are not afraid of water. Their fear comes from negative experiences or is sensed from their mother's attitude toward water and swimming. Similarly, a child who has never seen a dog will be unconcerned, and will walk up to it and pet it, but if his mother says, "Don't touch it, it'll bite you," the child will become frightened or at least wary.

All the mothers I have known, except the rare few, were terrified of giving their newborn baby the first bath at home.

Those mothers who handle their baby inexpertly and hesitantly affect the child adversely. If a mother knows what she is supposed to do and handles the child confidently, the child will benefit from that and be secure too. But of course no new mother is very expert to begin with. As for me though, after having my baby I could hardly wait to get home from the hospital to give her her first bath and begin the long road to swimming.

At the hospital, the nurses advised me to get into the routine of bathing the baby before the ten o'clock meal. I did this for about a week and then I had to do some serious reevaluation. The baby was yelling and screaming from the minute I undressed her to get her ready for her bath, and the planned playtime in the bath was nothing but a screaming session.

I intuited that she was crying so much because she was hungry. So I changed tactics and from then on I fed her at ten, let her rest for about ten to fifteen minutes while I got the bath ready, and then we started our daily fun session. It was a wonderful change: her belly was full, she was happy and completely relaxed in the water, and, boy, did she sleep after her bath!

In three weeks she was floating on her back, with a little support from me under her head. I made sure that she was in and under the water as much as possible. Lying on her back, her ears were completely submerged, and while I was holding her I would gently splash some water on her face. Neighbors and friends who came to see me at bath time were horrified.

"What are you doing to her? You'll kill her!"

"Don't worry, I know what I'm doing."

I must add, none of their children were swimming at a very early age.

GAMES AND PREPARATION IN THE BATHROOM

As soon as possible, transfer your baby from his usual baby bath to the family bathtub. Fill the bath about three inches deep so that when the baby lies flat on his back the water just comes past his ears. Gently splash some water over his face so he can get used to being wet all over.

If the phone rings don't answer it. If somebody is at the door ignore it. We constantly hear of tragic acci-

dents because of negligence. Remember, it only takes a few seconds for some disaster to occur, so *never* leave your baby alone in the bathtub. Try to organize your life so that you can spend a comfortable twenty minutes or more in the bathroom.

Make sure he has plenty of toys to play with, especially empty plastic bottles. He can fill them up with water and pour the water out, or just splash around with them.

When your baby is little he feels most comfortable lying on his back. Put your hands under his head to support him and gently move him backward and forward in the bath. As a baby grows he does more adventurous things in the bathtub. Teach him to kick his legs by first moving his legs for him to show how it is done. Your can also put your face in the water and show how to blow bubbles—but always come up smiling. Don't ever show panic. If your kiddie suddenly slips and disappears under the water, lift him out quickly, efficiently, and put a big smile on your face (even if your heart is beating two hundred times a minute), and say, "That was great! Will you show that to mommy again?" This way the child will assume that going under the water is fun and it's not something to be afraid of.

When letting the water out of the bath, don't have the baby there with you, as it often makes a loud noise that can frighten him.

Once babies master the art of sitting up, they seldom like to lie down again so this is a good time to introduce him to the shower. At first, alternate between having a shower and a bath. The water pressure in the shower should not be too strong, and he should have plenty of his favorite toys to play with, especially the empty plastic bottles.

Throughout the years, whenever I've run into a child in my class who is terrified of getting his face wet, I always hear the same story from the parent: "Oh no! . . . he never has a shower, he always has a tub bath and his face is washed with a cloth." If your child belongs in this category, my suggestion is, from this day on, switch to having showers and simply tell the child (wink, wink) the bathtub is broken.

Washing Hair the Easy Way

In many families washing hair is a dreaded occasion. Children yell, scream, and otherwise carry on. These are the ones who are not used to having their faces and ears completely wet and find it uncomfortable to go through the hair washing and rinsing process.

But if children are accustomed to being wet all over it won't upset them. Always use baby shampoo, which doesn't sting the eyes. (Don't use soap or your own brand of shampoo just because it happens to be handy.) The easiest way to wash hair is in the bath, in a sitting position; for rinsing, have them lie on their back. If children get used to the shower early enough, washing their hair under the shower should cause no problem.

Girls can take their dolls in the shower. Say, "You wash dolly's hair and I'll wash yours." For rinsing, tell them, "Stand right under the shower and rinse dolly's hair while I rinse your hair."

Another good game is to make all sorts of funny shapes with the lather, especially if they can see themselves in a mirror. Washing hair can be fun, if you make it that way.

BACKYARD POOLS

In many backyards and apartment complexes nowadays there is usually some form of a swimming pool. It can vary from a plastic eighteen-inch pool to a lavish deep tiled pool. If you have a backyard pool of any type I feel it is very important that children should be swimming on their own as soon as possible. If you don't own a boat or a swimming pool, or have some friends who do, you can leave teaching them to swim until they are five.

What Type of Pool to Build

If you are thinking of building a new pool, my advice is to provide a shallow end for the children. Even if those building the pool have no children, I would still advise providing a small area that is not deep and can be used for nonswimmers and young children.

If space permits, the most practical pool is a T-shaped one. One of the short ends of the T should be very shallow, from eighteen inches to two feet. The other short end of the T, for diving, should be eight feet deep, while the long end of the T will be used for swimming and should be about four feet deep.

The next best thing would be an L-shaped pool. The short end of the L shape could be built to cater to nonswimmers, and the long end of the L would have a continuous five-feet depth. If there is no room for spreading out, you should build fairly wide steps that can serve the purpose of a wading area.

I'm very much against building odd-shaped pools, the most popular being the kidney shape. They look very pretty and picturesque, but are completely useless. The only way you can swim in a kidney-shaped pool is around and around, like a goldfish.

Pool Safety for Children

If you are the proud owner of a swimming pool, you will soon discover that you have more friends (especially in the summer months) than you ever imagined—and a host of problems you didn't think of previously, such as what approach to take with your own nonswimming children, with the neighbors' children, and with your friends' children.

Before giving the okay for a swim for the children of neighbors and friends, give them a swimming test. Find out whether they can swim in the deep end. Can they tread water? Are *all* of them strong enough swimmers for you to feel confident? If the answer is yes, fine. If not, make sure that a reliable adult is around every moment while the children are in the pool.

Another good idea is to set aside certain times for public swimming. It makes life easy for you and your friends, since everyone knows when they can invade your pool.

But what to do with your own toddlers?

My advice: For most pool owners, the major problem is that they have to learn to live with danger. Don't, like most parents, tell the children all the time, "Don't go near the water, or you'll fall in and drown." All this does is teach them fear.

Instead, I would let them crawl and walk around the pool—when you're with them, of course, or close by to handle any emergency. If the child is too adventurous, and keeps getting into dangerous situations, I would eventually let him fall into the pool once, just long enough for him to drink two mouthfuls of water. Then say, "See, this is what mommy was talking about . . . this is what can happen to you." This is usually enough to teach children to be more careful.

Having a fence around any pool area is a necessity. Is this the only solution to water safety? *No!* I recently taught the surviving brother of a child who climbed through the hole dug by the family dog under the fence. Also, often the fence gate is not closed, whether through carelessness or a malfunction of a self-closing device. And children will even pile toys or whatever else is handy and can climb six-foot-high fences. Fencing is a barrier but not the solution.

The best answer is constant supervision, teaching the children how to swim, and having a good-quality fence around the pool with a self-closing gate. Learn cardiopulmonary resuscitation (CPR) and have a telephone at poolside.

DO'S AND DON'TS OF POOL SAFETY

DO constantly supervise pool activities—tragedy takes only a few seconds to occur.

DO erect a child-proof fence.

DO have a telephone in the pool area with emergency numbers visible.

DO post step-by-step CPR instructions near the pool.

DO leave large kicking boards and buoys in the pool, day and night.

DO have a designated nondrinking adult in charge of pool activities during social gatherings.

DO make sure your pool-cleaning equipment is keeping the water clear because in case of an accident, sometimes that can make the difference.

DON'T yell for help unless you really need it.

DON'T try to save a friend unless you are a strong swimmer. Run and find outside help.

DON'T ever dive into water of unknown depth.

DON'T push anybody into the water—adult or child.

DON'T rely on swimming aids (rubber rings, floaties, bubbles). They are not life preservers!

DON'T let children run, skip, fight, or ride three-wheelers around the water's edge.

What Type of Bathing Suits and Hair Length Are Best

When taking your baby into the swimming pool for the daily dip, the best thing for the baby to wear is nothing. But this is not always possible. Diapers are too bulky and heavy, so little bikini-type pants are the best—with or without protective covering.

You should pay close attention to the type of swimming suit your children wear because a lot of bad habits in swimming can be caused by the wrong type of suit. With some children I have known, I have had to battle to get their arms properly out of the water. Having constantly to pull their fallen shoulder straps back, they have grown accustomed to holding one arm under the water all the time, ready to fix the strap.

I'm therefore personally very much against having those horrid two-piece suits on little girls. The top part usually slips up around their necks, and the shoulder straps are always falling down.

Children who swim can rarely afford the luxury of having long hair. For boys, the hair must not come down past their eyebrows. For girls, the same applies, and if they have shoulder-length hair, it should be tied up, either in a ponytail or two pigtails, so that when they come up for air the hair doesn't interfere with their breathing. Bobby pins are a nuisance. They don't stay in place and all swimming pool owners hate the sight of them. Many types of pool bottoms are discolored by rusting bobby pins. And even if the pool is tiled, it's a nuisance picking them up.

Swimming Aids

There are many types of swimming aids available, all of which have their useful purposes. **WARNING:** A nonswimmer should not rely on a swimming aid unless he is familiar with water.

A lot of parents are reluctant to provide them, thinking their children will become dependent on them. Fortunately, this is not so. When children feel confident enough, they will discard them, just as they discard their milk bottles and pacifiers. The usefulness of each swimming aid will be discussed more fully in a later chapter, but here is a brief description of each.

KICKING BOARD
There are many varieties and shapes of kicking boards—polyfoam, smooth plastic, wood, fiberglass. Try to get the smallest and thinnest, because children can hold on to them much easier.

FLOATS

A bubble float is a block of polyfoam with a belt attached that is buckled around the child's waist. The inflatable variety can be dangerous as they can puncture easily, so avoid them. Unfortunately, most of the designs are not perfect. As the child progresses with swimming instruction and requires less assistance, the block of polyfoam can be cut down as needed (an electric carving knife is ideal). When purchasing one, look for a strong child-proof plastic buckle to avoid rust. When you put a bubble on, don't tie it too tight around the tummy; leave about a two-finger space between the strap and the flesh. The water lifts the bubble up, and if the strap is tied too tightly it will cut into the child and be uncomfortable. If the bubble belt strap has a loose end, always tie a tight knot in it for extra safety.

FLOATIES

Floatie armbands come in many shapes and price ranges. Try to find ones that are not too bulky, as the bulky ones can restrict arm movement. Floatie armbands are not recommended for use with children under the age of three. However, extended use of floaties can create bad swimming habits later on.

FLIPPERS

Flippers can be very useful, and children love them, but they are the only swimming aid which can be overused and the only one they don't want to get rid of.

In early learning stages flippers can be helpful, but make sure that on every occasion the child wears them there is an equal amount of time swimming without them. If you find that your child gets too dependent on the flippers, lose one, and if it's necessary, lose the other as well.

In the chapter on the five-to-ten age group, I will explain in detail the advantages and disadvantages of the flipper kick.

SNORKELS

Snorkels and face masks can be dangerous in swimming pools. The face mask can be too large and rigid, and if the child accidentally bumps into the wall it can cause injury. But they are great fun at the beach.

GOGGLES

Goggles have become popular in the last decade, as the heavy chlorination in pools has created an understandable demand for eye protection. The most expensive ones are not necessarily the best since they are usually designed for adults. The critical things to look for are a size that will fit the face of the child and a molded soft plastic seal around the eyes, preferably in one piece. To test the fit, try pressing the goggles on the child's face to see if they create the necessary sealed vacuum around the eyes. I recommend wearing goggles after the age of three.

There are many other water-related gadgets available, from inflatable vests to baby-seat floating devices. Inflatable vests can be useful for some handicapped people. Very dangerous, however, are all inflatable toys such as buoys, ducks, swans, and so forth.

ASTHMA AND SWIMMING

Although swimming doesn't cure asthma, by now, it's a well-known fact that asthma sufferers get great relief when they take up swimming. More and more doctors realize this and are sending children for swimming lessons.

How much help children experience depends on what age they contract asthma. The younger they are, the more chance they have of significantly recovering.

Why is swimming so helpful? Because it expands the lungs and teaches regular rhythmic breathing. Also, instead of doing boring breathing exercises, the children have fun while they swim—they don't realize that while they're having fun they are helping themselves to get better. But just blowing bubbles into the water doesn't help much; breathing must be synchronized with regular, correct swimming strokes. This is where heated swimming pools are essential because children, and adults, can practice throughout the year.

If you have a two-year-old who suffers from asthma, it could be one year (because of his undeveloped physical coordination) before the swimming is beneficial. Keep in mind, though, teaching an asthmatic child to swim usually takes longer than it would another child: because of their breathing disability they have a justified fear of holding their face under the water. It takes a little more time and patience as well as an understanding instructor.

DISABLED CHILDREN AND SWIMMING

If a handicapped or disabled child learns to swim, it not only helps him physically but it gives a tremendous boost to his ego. I can't think of any other sport in which somebody with one leg, say, could compete on equal terms with other people. In my native Hungary, there was a very famous long-distance swimmer who had lost one leg but was National Champion for many years. In swimming, the kicking of the legs is not all that important; it serves as a balance to the arms. So if someone is without a leg, they achieve the necessary balance by kicking with their one leg. Usually they develop very strong muscles in their upper body and that often compensates for the lack of full leg movement.

Learning to swim often builds a real sense of confidence. Slow learners at school can become excellent pupils after they have mastered the art of swimming. I have known a few children who had severe stutters. After they came to me and began swimming, they reduced their stuttering so much they did not need to continue speech therapy.

I have found no problem at all with hearing-impaired children. If anything, they make better pupils; they constantly keep their eyes on my lips and follow what I'm saying—unlike some rambunctious darlings.

When teaching disabled children or adults, you must use great imagination and be flexible. Make use of the capabilities they have, even if the result is not picture perfect. Teacher and pupil can gain great satisfaction from the result.

SHOULD YOU DEMONSTRATE?

Don't ever *demonstrate* swimming to the children. I know this will shock many people, but children find it overwhelming, even frightening, to see an adult swim-

ming, and they can't comprehend the rapid movements. Could you watch a golf pro or tennis star demonstrate excellent performance and then immediately duplicate their performance?

The only time I ever demonstrated swimming was at the very beginning of my teaching career. I came to the swimming pool every day, got a beautiful suntan, and waited and waited for my first pupil to materialize. Madaline, a lovely old Australian lady with weathered skin who obviously had spent her life at this particular rock pool by the beach, must have taken pity on me. She asked why I was at the pool sun bathing every day. I told her of my previous competitive past, and I said now that I have stopped competitive swimming I would like to teach children. The only problem was I needed a first pupil. A few minutes later, an unsuspecting vacationing couple with children walked in. Madaline whispered into my ear, "Eva, go and start swimming. . . ." I swam as beautifully as I could—even outdoing Esther Williams. Meanwhile, Madaline glided over to the couple and said, "Looooook at that girl swim! Isn't that beauuuuutiful? Wouldn't you like your children to learn to swim like that?" In awe, the parents answered, "Yes!" Madaline waved to me . . . I got out—and I had my first pupils. But I never swam in front of my students again.

THE IMPORTANCE OF DISCIPLINE AND REWARDS

Discipline is a *must* during swimming lessons. If I tell a child to sit on the steps, I expect the child to stay there while I have my back turned.

How do I achieve that? It is done by laying out the rules and sticking to them. I make a big fuss about my reward system during the first lesson. I work with rubber stamps and jelly beans—one jelly bean to be exact. My trademark is a smiling face. If you are good, you get one stamp on the back of the hand. If you really listen and try hard, two stamps (one on each hand). If you are fantastic, maybe three stamps (the third on the forehead). During the lesson I give progress reports, saying things like, "Gee, that was really a good try. So far, you have earned two smiling faces." Sometimes, halfway through the lesson I might say, "You are not listening; you haven't earned your stamps yet—not even one." It can also happen that the child was terrible that day and I would say, "No smiling face today and you will only get half a jelly bean." With proper theatrics I bite a small jelly bean in half and as I'm giving it to him say, "Next time I see you, I hope I can give you a full jelly bean and a stamp too."

In over thirty years of teaching, it has never happened that the child who got a half jelly bean didn't try his very best the next lesson. I am very strict and consistent about this reward system and the children very quickly respond to it and behave. If the child does something extraordinarily brave, like overcoming his fear and jumping into the water for the first time, he gets the "tummy job"—a smiling face on the belly. This is the equivalent of winning a gold medal, and after all the fuss and praise, they treasure it and show it to everybody.

Sometimes I also write love letters, as I call them, on very colorful note paper.

   Dear Eli,
   Thank you for putting your face in the water today.
                              Love, Eva xxx

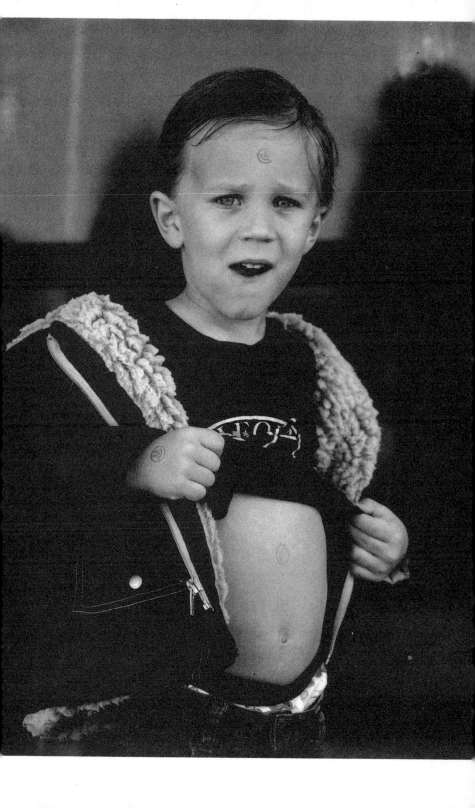

Dear Richard,

I couldn't believe that you stopped crying today. Thank you so much.

Love, Eva xxx

Recently a newspaper reporter observed my classes and later reported on the NO TEARS SWIM SCHOOL I was running. I came to the conclusion a long time ago that I can't stand crying children. A crying child is not going to learn, so we are both wasting our time. I have figured out that they cry for only two reasons: either they are being naughty or they are being fearful. I act accordingly, and approach each situation individually. I usually explain my rules for the naughty children: "You are allowed to cry, but you are not allowed to kick me." I even encourage the crying child by saying, "I love the way you cry, could you do it a bit louder?" After hearing this response from me, they soon stop crying just to spite me. When this happens, I say, "Don't stop crying, I really love it!" They almost always say "No!"

For the fearful child, I give a lot of sympathy and lots of hugs. "I don't like this, I want my mommy, I want to go home!" I reply, "I know how you feel, I would like to have my mommy, too. But, sometimes we have to try things we might not like at first. I will hold you, and I won't let you go. Let's just do a little bit of kicking and very soon you can go home." They stop crying, and in the process they fall in love with me. Then we get on with the lessons.

Parents need to set rules and then stick to them, even if it involves saying no. Spending time in the water with your child is a wonderful experience. Just make sure that it is a happy and safe time by exercising common sense and proper discipline.

2

SUPER BABIES (FOUR MONTHS TO WALKING AGE)

Yes, young babies can be taught to swim. Actually, it's not swimming as we all know it. It's floating, and there is a fair amount of controversy surrounding its usefulness and its benefits. Teaching babies is not for everyone, and you should read this chapter thoroughly to decide if you and your baby really are ready for this long-term commitment.

The way I teach babies is not uniquely my technique as it is with other age groups. The original idea wasn't mine, but over the years I have worked on it and made it as pleasant as possible for both the child and the parent.

The first question any reasonable person would ask is: Why should a four-month-old baby learn to swim? It can't walk, so why on earth should it swim?

Babies have a tendency to grow up, and in no time they reach the toddler age where they not only walk, but run, touch everything in sight, and are very curious. They see a body of shining, inviting water. They reach out to touch the sunshine shimmering on the water, or a floating toy; or they lose their balance and fall in. If they have been taught as young babies how to fall in and come up to the surface floating on their backs, they _can survive_. Otherwise, they could become a number in the horrifying statistics of children drowning under the age of five.

In 1987, the American Academy of Pediatrics came out publicly against children learning to swim until the age of three. Their reasoning is that children learn to perform only under controlled situations, usually a coordination of routines between parent and child, so in emergency situations, children won't know how to react. Wrong. With my teachings, countless mothers have gratefully reported to me that John had fallen in and come up—floated—and thus survived.

There is further controversy about the child developing ear and nose trouble and the adverse effects of drinking infectious water. If your child is not healthy or has a tendency to get earaches, make sure the child doesn't take a swimming class.

In 1987 my good friend and mentor, the famous Australian Olympic swimming coach, Forbes Carlile, visited the then Soviet Union for the third time. What impressed him most was that the Soviets were adding small indoor pools to their numerous polyclinics (multi-purpose health clinics) throughout the country. Many installed bathtubs instead of pools, where trained personnel show parents how to exercise babies in water. The Soviets believe that healthy bodies create healthy minds, and they have recognized that swimming is the perfect exercise to be practiced from very early age to very old age. Forbes showed me a videotape of young babies—as young as twenty-one days—being exercised in the bathtub. Between the ban in America by some doctors and the government's blessing in the Soviet Union, what is the truth? What should you, as a caring parent, do?

The decision is yours.

When a parent calls my swimming school and asks about my superbaby class, I ask why he or she wants to have the baby taught to swim. If they have a backyard pool, it makes sense to want to teach the baby. If they don't, I point out that there is no immediate danger, and they should wait until the baby is fifteen to eighteen months old. I tell them that it can take up to three months to learn, and that after the baby has mastered the floating, they have to keep up the skill all year around, at least once a week, otherwise it's not worth starting. Before the lessons commence, I ask the parents to come to my school and observe a class, so they can decide if they want to make that commitment or not.

As a responsible teacher, I carefully select my pupils and their parents. You, as a responsible parent, should weigh the consequences and decide for yourself if you want your baby to learn to float at an early age or not.

When teaching infants, the best age to start is when they are three to four months old. If your child is already walking, regardless of age, forget it. A ten-month-old baby is not going to be happy lying on his back. His motor skills have developed to the point where he can sit up and walk. So naturally he is not going to be happy staying stationary. He wants to see what's going on around him. On the other hand, if the baby has already learned the trick of floating by the age of seven- to eight months, he doesn't know any other alternative. He will stay put quite happily and without a struggle.

Some swimming organizations accept children to what they call survival classes even up to the age of three years. Those children are forcibly, sometimes cruelly, taught to float on their backs. The children protest; they fight it by attempting to turn onto their stomachs; they scream. If this is the case, yes, it can be a very traumatic experience, and no, they shouldn't be put through the unnecessary and unproductive suffering.

I know from my own experience that motherly feelings and common sense are not God given, and one has, especially with one's first child, a lot of doubt. "Am I doing the right thing? Should I do this and this?" Use your own judgment deciding how far you want to push your child.

If you are thinking of joining a local swimming class, my advice is, as it is with all other age groups, go and observe first. If the children are happy and are laughing (yes, babies can laugh), fine. If the children cry, seem uncomfortable, are shivering from cold, and throw up, turn on your heel and leave.

The pool preferably should be indoors, the water clear, the classes small, and, generally speaking, there should be a relaxed atmosphere.

TEACHING YOUR BABY AT HOME—PRELIMINARY LESSONS

If, however, you decide to do your own teaching at home, here is what the first lesson should consist of:

▶ Enter the water, holding the baby firmly in your arms. Walk around the pool. Let the baby get used to the surroundings. Take your time. Gently, with your hand, wash the baby down, and as you are walking slowly, holding the baby still firmly in your arms, lower yourself and the baby fully into the water so you are both wet up to your necks.

▶ Change position by holding the baby in front of you, thumbs curling around the baby's shoulders.

▶ Try to cup your wrists together so the baby's chin is resting on your wrist. This prevents the baby's head from flopping into the water and keeps him from inadvertently drinking water.

▶ When you both feel comfortable, start walking backwards, constantly looking at your baby's face, and gently bouncing the baby up and down.

▶ After a few minutes, change the holding position. Turning the baby on its back, place the baby's head on your shoulder so it rests comfortably. You should be so close that you are touching cheek to cheek. Firmly, with your left hand, hold the baby's bottom; with your right hand, support the baby's upper body. Start walking backwards, gently bouncing and constantly talking to the baby in a reassuring voice. If you run out of things to say, you can recite a song, a poem, or what you did yesterday. It doesn't matter what you say. It's the tone of voice that matters.

► As the baby settles down, use your judgment as to when to lower your shoulders into the water so the baby's ears are fully submerged. After a few minutes, pick the baby up, kiss her, and tell her, with a big smile, how clever she is.

Now comes the big step for both of you.

► Very firmly, touch and support the baby's head under the water with your right hand. With your left hand, hold the baby's bottom, but this time the baby will be in front of you, and the top of the head is supported by your breast. The baby is the long end of a T. Keep your face over the baby's head and, again, slowly walk backwards, gently bouncing up and down.

By now you have three variations of exercises: facing the baby, supporting her chin; her head resting on your shoulder; and holding her out in front of you.

Repeat these three exercises, using your discretion as to how long to continue with each. Fifteen to twenty minutes in the water is enough.

Your next lessons should follow the same pattern as the first, getting wet gently, facing the baby for a short while, and then turning her on her back. This time you can introduce two more important exercises.

► Holding the baby at arm's length, your fingers firmly around her armpits and rib cage, blow onto her face. Say "Swim," and without hesitation gently push her vertically under the water. It shouldn't be more than ten centimeters, or three inches, under the water. This should take a few seconds. Try to be calm, don't rush it, don't jerk the baby out too fast. When the baby comes up, tell her again how proud you are of her.

At this stage, don't put the baby underwater more than three times, and certainly not one time after the other. By blowing on her face, she will hold on to her breath, and by repetition she will learn that when she hears "Swim," she will automatically take a breath to hold the air, because she knows that she will go under the water.

The next major exercise is very important too, because this will create the major breakthrough of learning to float on her own.

▶ Standing still, hold the baby's hand with one hand, and with the other support her under her back. Slowly and gently, relax your hand under the baby's head and start stroking her head under the water. Ever so gently, take your hand away, but hold it ready in a cupped form two to three inches away from her head. In the beginning, tap and stroke her head every five to ten seconds, and when the baby gets used to the idea that she can hold her head on her own, the tappings should decrease.

TEACHING YOUR BABY AT HOME—YOUR BABY CAN FLOAT

Next time you are in the water, and when you feel secure that the baby is comfortable and relaxed, do the following:

▶ Hold and support her head, and let her body float without supporting her under her back. Change smoothly from supporting her head only to supporting her back only. The best way to understand this balancing act is to imagine that you are tossing a large volume of feathers. After a while, you will feel that your baby doesn't need your support, and is capable of floating on her own.

It's not possible to give you a time frame on how long it will take to achieve this. If you go into the water every day and spend twenty minutes exercising with her, she could be floating in six weeks, or it might take three months. A lot depends on how old the baby is, how you work as a team, how favorable the conditions are (warm water is best), and whether the routine is continuous. Children learn by repetition, and I have seen many times that even a weekly break from lessons can cause a setback.

If the baby is constantly unhappy in the water, try to pacify her. If this uneasiness persists for a few lessons, then swimming lessons are not for her. You might start again when she is about eighteen months.

WATER SAFETY FOR BABIES

The two basics that the baby has to learn are how to hold her breath underwater, and how to float. When she has mastered these two important steps, you finish the lessons off by teaching her how to behave if she falls into the pool.

Sit the baby on the edge of the pool and face her. Cross your hands, holding on to her arms. When you say "Go," pull the baby into the water by uncrossing your arms, which means that your baby will hit the water on her back. By this time, your baby has learned to hold her breath when she hits the water. She has also learned how to float, so she will come up and float by herself.

Remember:

Repeat each exercise each day.

Skip an exercise if the baby has mastered it.

Keep a clock by the side of the pool, and time the

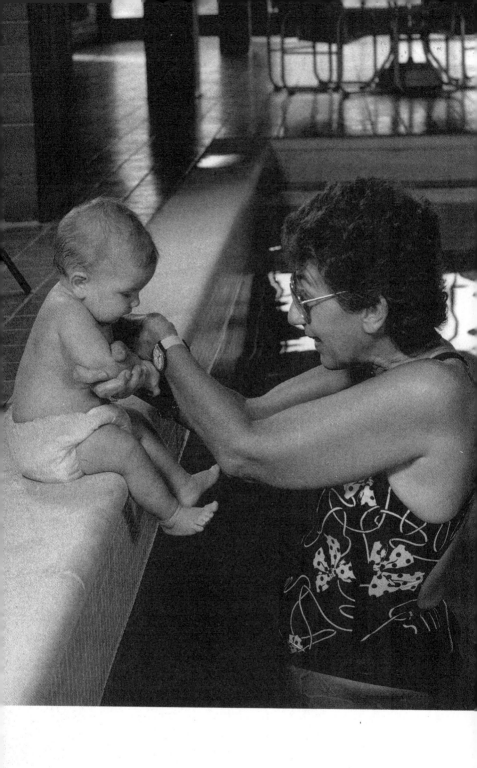

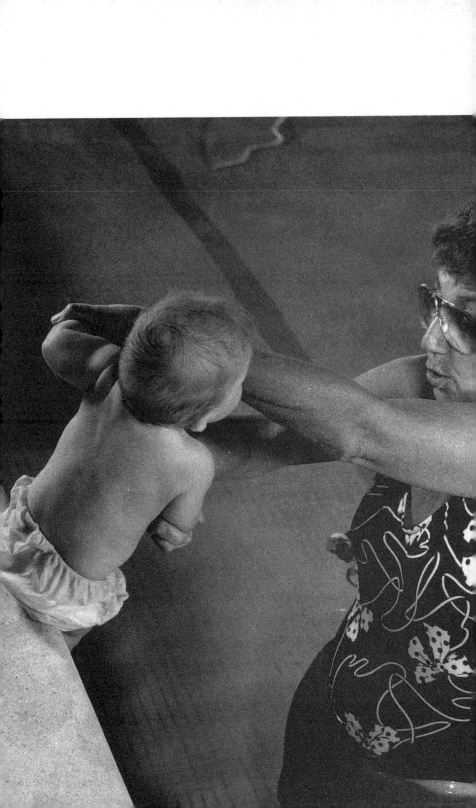

baby's floating time, from thirty seconds to a maximum of ten minutes.

Your baby will not "perform" each day. Some days she will be on strike. Gently and patiently go through the routines, shortening some, lengthening others.

SOME COMMONSENSE SUGGESTIONS AND SIGNS OF DISTRESS TO LOOK OUT FOR

- ▶ Don't feed her milk prior to the lesson.
- ▶ Don't overtire your baby.
- ▶ Rigid, curled (clawlike) fists are a sign the baby is in distress.
- ▶ White above the upper lip indicates that the baby has swallowed too much air or water. Stop, pick her up, and burp her.
- ▶ A tight, swollen belly is a sign that the baby has swallowed too much water. Burp her, try to take her to the potty. If the belly stays drum-tight, stop the lessons.
- ▶ Crying. Babies will cry for many reasons. As a parent, you can tell the difference between an "I don't feel like doing this" cry and a "Help me, I'm very uncomfortable" cry.
- ▶ Whimpering is okay. Desperate crying is not okay.

YES! BABIES CAN LEARN TO FLOAT!

I know it works. Way back in 1975 in Sydney, Australia, we were all excited at my swimming school because a British TV crew from the BBC came over to film floating babies. The big day came. The director didn't want eleven-month-old Fiona's mother to be there to pull her into the water. He wanted Fiona to fall in on her own. We sat Fiona down at the edge of the pool and urged her to jump in by herself. Since she was well trained not to do it on her own, she just sat there with bemusement on her face, seeming to think, "Why are they all yelling, 'Fiona, jump, jump!' " I suggested to the director that we ask Fiona's five-year-old brother, Roger, to push her in. After all, in real life a situation like this can occur. So Roger walked up to Fiona, and with all his might, without any warning, he shoved her in. Camera whirling, everybody waiting for Fiona to come up—but no Fiona. Just as I was readying to jump in to help her,

she appeared on the top of the water, crying, but floating beautifully.

The force of Roger's push was a surprise for her, and it must have taken her a few more seconds, which to us seemed like an eternity, to come up to the surface. Everybody was clapping—the director, crew, and other parents present.

And for me, that was the first true realization that babies can truly learn to float.

3

*W*ALKING AGE TO THREE YEARS

When I get a phone call from a parent who wants to enroll a thirteen-month-old baby in one of my swimming classes, I explain to him that I can't do much teaching at that age. I explain that soon after the baby learns to walk, the parent can do more with the child than I can. Also, a child who has just started to walk will only kick in the water when he feels like kicking, and I won't take any money for lessons that do not achieve results. The parent and child can join my classes when the child has reached the "mature" age of fifteen to eighteen months.

As I've discussed earlier, if the child has started lessons at four months, then there is no problem. The child has learned to float on his back, and provided that the practice is continued all year round, that knowledge is remembered even if he reaches two years of age. There is also no problem if the child has had its bathroom routine practice, is familiar with the water, and is used to having his ears, eyes, nose, and mouth wet.

The aim of my parent-and-child class is to make the children safe in case they happen to fall into the pool. This involves going under the water, continuous kicking and arm movements, and certainly being able to get from point A to point B. They are also taught how to climb out of the pool.

If you are beginning the child's first water experience at walking age, don't be discouraged if little is achieved. Follow the instructions prescribed in this chapter but don't expect great results. The time you spend in the water with your child is not wasted: When their little bodies and minds are ready to take it all in, they will eventually follow your instructions.

Don't ever compare your child's ability with another's. Some children will start walking at nine months and some will walk as late as fifteen months. Some children can be good swimmers at three years of age, while some children can be good swimmers at four years of age.

Let's start with the lesson.

Hold the child firmly in your arms so you are facing each other, and enter the water, holding him in an upright position. Make sure that you are familiar with the pool's depth and that you can always walk without slipping and be able to hold him comfortably without losing your grip. The ideal pool depth is 3 feet six inches to three feet nine inches.

Walk across the pool, and while holding him firmly, lower yourself so that both of you can get wet. You can gently wash the child's face.

Hold the child under his arms in front of you so that you can see his face *all the time*. Remember, you, the teacher, have to walk backwards, *always, every time,* because it is the child who is swimming forward.

Place the child's arms around your neck and get hold of his knees from under the water.

Walking backwards, start moving his legs up and down and constantly repeat, "Kick, kick, kick." Don't say phrases like "Now, be a good boy and show mommy how you can move your legs." Just say, "Kick, kick, kick."

Every movement has a name; arm movements are going to be called "Paddle, paddle"; blowing bubbles will be "Bubble, bubble"; and if you want his mouth closed, it will be a simple "Mmmmm." These children are very young and you should cut down the verbal instructions as much as possible. They learn by you physically showing them what is required, and as you will see, all the separate little exercises come together at the end.

After the kicking (maybe four times across the pool), start walking backwards and blow, giving a raspberry on the arm or even on the chest. Blowing the bubbles will tickle him and he can feel the vibration. As you blow each round of bubbles, say, "Bubble, bubble."

BOBBING

Still holding him under the arms, and still walking backwards, gently start lifting him up and down, higher and higher. If you are brave you can slightly toss him into the air, always making sure that he lands in firm hands with a firm grip. This game is good for both of you, and when you realize that you can let him go, it is great fun. At this stage, his face might even get wet, which is fine, but he won't even realize this.

Go back to the kicking, this time holding him out at arm's length away from you. Your shoulders have to be under the water and both of your faces just out of the water. Now say again: "Peter, kick, kick, kick," and, miracle of miracles, he will do it. It could be a frog kick, it could be a bent knee kick—whatever it is, don't correct his natural kick. You might want to tip him a little bit from side to side. It usually helps things along.

PADDLING

Now, lean against the wall and have him sit on your lap facing away from you. Put your hand on top of his hands and start moving his arms forward in a circular

motion, saying, "Paddle, paddle." Make sure that your hand is on top of his and that he has the freedom to feel the water pressing against his little hands. There should be no splash.

The following is difficult. Start walking backwards again, but this time hold on to his hands. You are both paddling, you in a reverse mode, and he moving his arms forward. Very likely, he is not going to kick, so just prop his body up with one of your legs under the water. Hop backwards on one leg, while with a cheerful smile saying, "Paddle, paddle, paddle." The first time you do this, you think only a circus acrobat can do it, but after a while you will get used to it and be able to do it easily.

When dealing with a very young child, don't say, "Paddle and kick your legs and blow bubbles." One instruction at a time.

FOR SAFETY—HOLDING ON TO THE WALL

If you have another person with you in the water, you can do the next exercise with his or her help. If not, move to the wall. The distance should be not further than one yard. Let's assume that you are working at the pool wall by yourself.

Hold the child under the armpits, but this time hold him by your side. Put your fingers under his arms in order to prop his arms out straight in front of him. Say, "Ready, go" and gently ease him to the wall. Make sure that he holds on to the wall by himself. If he is too small to hold on, wrap your fingers around his and let him stay there. While you are holding on, introduce the wall and say, "Wall, wall."

Repeat this four or five times.

Still standing and facing the wall, do the same: "Ready, go," and then say, "Paddle, paddle" and gently push him to the wall so that at the end he holds on to the wall.

Repeat this four or five times.

Still standing facing the wall, say, "Ready, go, kick, kick" and gently push him to the wall.

Repeat this about four or five times.

At this stage, his head is out of the water, but his chin and mouth should be in the water.

If you stick to the routine, after a few repetitions, he will know that at "ready" he has to take a breath, because when he hears "go," he knows that you mean business and that he will be let go.

As you are both getting better and better at doing this, after a few lessons, instead of holding him by your side, as you let him "swim" to the wall, he can be in front of you as you ease him to the wall by putting your middle finger into the back of his head, just at the nape of the neck. There is a hollow spot there, I think made just for this purpose.

Putting It All Together

Now comes the last part of the lesson: jumping, turning, swimming back to the wall, and climbing out.

Sit the child on the edge of the pool, face him with a big smile on your face, and say: "Now Peter is going to jump." Firmly holding on to his arms or hands, making sure you are completely in charge of the situation, say, "Ready, go" and pull him in immediately. Unless he is a total tadpole, don't put his face under the water but slowly turn him around and push him back to the wall. Say, "Back to the wall."

Now turn him around to face the side of the pool. Place one of his elbows onto the deck, then place the other elbow on the deck, and, holding his bottom, push him up so that he gets out of the water by himself. As you do it, say, "Elbow, elbow, knee."

I have a rubber doll. I've had her for years. She and I have grown old together in the water. I put the doll next to the child and say: "Watch the dolly, it's going to jump. Ready, go; paddle, paddle, kick, kick, back to the wall, elbow, elbow, knee." I know it sounds like pidgin English, but the eighteen-month- to three-year-old crowd appreciates it.

As the lessons go on (never, never more than thirty minutes in duration), the child will learn to take a breath at "ready" and hold his breath at "go," so at this point you can let him go under the water. In the beginning, do this just once during the lesson and then slowly increase the number of times you do it as you are progressing. Don't get carried away with this activity, because you as a grown-up don't realize that a little bit of exercise is a lot of exercise for a small child.

Be careful always regarding the amount of water taken in. There are two signs to watch for: one is a drum-tight belly and the other is a whiteness over the upper lip. If either of these occurs, pick him up and burp him like a young baby.

Remember when you had to walk backwards like a circus acrobat? As the child progresses you can let him go as you walk backwards and while he swims under the water, bend down and give your instructions, "Paddle, paddle, kick, kick." Children can hear underwater. The hardest thing for them to learn is to lift their faces out of the water. You will work out a routine where you will know how long the child can comfortably hold his breath. Lift him up, let him take a big breath, and gently ease him in again. Just follow the child's natural breathing pattern. Little children will automatically open their eyes under water. They can see your legs as well as your bathing suit, and are reassured you are still there. If the child is not swimming on top of the water, but sinks down like a rock, the fault is yours. He should be in a horizontal position before you let him go.

I have known some two-year-olds who when swimming take a breath and completely disappear to the bottom of the pool. They then work themselves up to the top of the water for a breath and down they go again. For unsuspecting onlookers, this would be a frightening sight, but these children are confident in the water and no harm will come to them. At the very early stage, style and beauty don't come into it, only confidence, fun, familiarity with the water—and safety.

If you are doing the lessons with a partner, for the first six lessons, only one adult should handle the child. The partner can be involved in exercises, like tossing the child from one to another. When I am conducting a parent-and-child class, in the beginning I hardly touch the child and I explain and show certain holds by having my faithful doll with me in the water. All instructors (whether parent or professional) touch differently, have different emphases on words, and I don't want to confuse the children by having them passed from one teacher to another. The partner can also be involved when you say, "Peter is going to fly to daddy . . . one, two, three, go. . . ." Notice, I said, "One, two, three, go" and *not* "One, two, three, ready go." "Ready, go," is reserved strictly for swimming and jumping.

I usually finish the lessons with a rousing rendition of "Hokey, Pokey." Holding the child in your lap, you could sing any song that is familiar as long as you sing and dance and make a big splash and both of you have a good time.

The reason I did not include any work while on their back is because at this age they do not particularly like lying on their back. If you have one who does like it, please read the chapter on babies, where there is a detailed description.

TO SUMMARIZE:

First part of the lesson:
kicking
bobbing
bubbling
paddling
Total time: seven minutes

Second part of the lesson at the wall or with a partner:
floating with arms stretched out
kicking
paddling
kicking and paddling
holding on to the wall
Total time: seven minutes

Third part of the lesson at the wall:
jumping
going underwater and coming up for air
turning
kicking and paddling to the wall
climbing out—"Elbow, elbow, knees"
Total time: seven minutes

Game for five minutes

4

THREE-TO FIVE-YEAR-OLDS

TEACHING THEM YOURSELF

If you yourself want to take up teaching, start off with a small number of pupils. Bad-tempered teachers can do more harm than good. When teaching, don't strive for absolute perfection. The most important thing is the children's happiness and willingness to learn. We can and should all become teachers of something if we are to consider ourselves responsible adults.

How many children should be in the class?

If you are not experienced or if you are unsure of yourself, start off with two. I think for an experienced teacher the ideal number is four children in the class.

When dealing with preschool children, it is much better for them to have company while they are learning something. If you have just one child, he or she will tire quickly and the concentration span will be very short indeed. The ideal situation would be to have a half-hour lesson, followed by a half hour of play.

Whether you can afford to let the children romp around depends on the size of the pool. When there are, say, four children in the class, they all have to take their turn. While one gets personal instruction from you, the other three are either resting or playing or practicing. This way, out of the half hour, each child gets about seven minutes of individual instruction. That doesn't sound like much, but even if you kept them in the water for two hours, they would still only be receptive for about seven to ten minutes.

If the pool is outdoors, even if the weather is fine, you will soon find that the children will start shivering and turning blue after twenty minutes in the water. It's a funny thing about children, that while they are having a lesson, they tend to get cold and miserable quickly, but the moment you utter the magic words, "It's playtime," the face that was blue a minute before turns a rosy red. The same child can stay in the water for practically an unlimited time, just playing.

While children are in class, they don't move around very much, and in the early stages of learning they are scared, which is the reason for their shivering. The same child who was getting cold when you first started to teach him will stop this after a few lessons when he has gained some confidence.

If it is a slightly windy day, keep their shoulders under the water right through the lesson.

Make it a rule that they never get wet before lesson time. Don't let children in the water before the start of the lesson, even if it's a hot and sunny 90 degree day, because if they have their play first, they are completely useless and worn out for their lesson.

Before entering the water, make sure that all children have gone to the toilet and have blown their noses. Be very strict about not letting them have anything in their mouths such as candy and especially chewing gum. If a child looks suspect, ask him to open his mouth so you can examine it. If there is anything in the mouth, it not only distracts their attention, but they can easily bite their tongue.

If you teach very young children you must be prepared to go into the water with them. Even if the teaching takes place in the shallow end of the pool, you must be right there. If the weather is not to your liking and you don't feel like going in, better to cancel the lesson than stay outside the pool giving instructions.

Avoid Big Words and Try to Think as a Child Would

When teaching, don't use big words. Always remember that your pupils are preschool age. I remember years ago, I was teaching a four-year-old, Julie, to float on her back. She was stiff as an ironing board, and I kept on whispering into her ear, "Relax, Julie, relax." She looked back at me with a blank, uncomprehending look, and it dawned on me that she didn't know what I was talking about. After the lesson, I went over to her father and asked him would he, when they got home, try to explain to her what the word "relax" means.

Next morning Julie turned up with a big grin on her face, and when I asked her, "Do you know what 'relax' means?" she threw herself with a big dramatic movement on the floor, holding her arms and legs indeed in a very relaxed way, eyes closed. I congratulated her on her performance and turned to her father: "How did you do it?"

He said, "We were watching TV last night and every time a bad guy was shot down, I said to Julie, 'See, this is how you relax.' "

From that day on I have never used the word "relax"; instead I say, "Let yourself go, softly, loose, be a rag doll, be like Jell-O." It works.

I noticed the passage of the years when recently I was talking to a four-year-old, explaining how to do a dolphin kicking by using the illustration "Do it like Flipper, on television." She looked at me with wide eyes and said, "Kick like the Mermaid?" I laughingly said, "Yes, of course." Try to use illustrations the child will be familiar with.

Four-year-olds don't understand words like "submerge," "surface," "exhale," "inhale"; use phrases like "go under," "come up," "blow out," "take a big breath." Don't forget, don't lose patience if you have to repeat the same thing a hundred times. When giving an instruction, always use the same phrase, the same words; even the facial expressions should be the same. If you say, "Take a big breath," always take a big breath yourself, overemphasizing the opening of the mouth.

BEGINNING THE CLASSES

The first and most important thing you have to do is to gain these little strangers' confidence. After all, they are going to place their lives in your hands, and you, being a grown-up, should know that it is not an easy thing to trust a stranger. If you are running regular classes, it's a good idea to ask the parents to bring their children once or twice to watch you giving another class before the new children are due to have their first lesson with you. The children then have an opportunity to size you up, get used to your voice, and see how a swimming lesson is run.

The first time a child comes to your class, tell him your name and ask him what his name is, even if you

know it. If the child readily answers and has a conversation with you, you shouldn't expect too much trouble from him. If she doesn't say a word but is quite willing to walk with you to the edge of the pool, she will be a slow starter but later will blossom into a willing pupil. Yet another one will be crying softly, not making too much of a fuss but letting the world know that she is not terribly happy. And then, of course, there will be the screamer, the yeller, the grabber. Let's call the first one Adam, the second Beth, the third Cathy, and the screamer David.

SITTING ON THE EDGE OF THE POOL AND KICKING

Take Adam's and Beth's hands and start walking in the shallow part of the pool. Keep talking all the time. Keep asking Beth her name, whether she has any brothers or sisters, if she has a pet in the house, if she goes to kindergarten, what her teacher's name is, and so on. Sooner or later you will find a subject that is close to her heart and the minute she starts talking to you, you are friends.

While you are trying to make friends with Adam and Beth, sit Cathy on the edge of the pool, keeping an eye on her, but look as if you are ignoring her completely, as if you don't even know she is sitting there. Pick up David, drag him away from mother, and make him sit next to Cathy. By this time Cathy has stopped whimpering and the appearance of David and his screaming makes her start all over again. If David has a bad case of hysterics he might even run back to mother again, so the performance will have to be repeated.

With Adam and Beth now friends, sit on the edge of the pool, with David and Cathy on each side of you, holding David's hand firmly, not so much for emotional support but rather to hold him back from running to mother again. Start kicking your legs gently in the water. Ask the group if anyone can kick their legs similarly. At the first attempt, guess who is going to imitate you? Adam of course. At this stage, get in the pool and stand in front of the children and say, "When I say go, start kicking again." Even if the splashing is very little, in mock horror say, "Children, please don't splash me!," after which they'll all start splashing like mad. For the first time you can see a devilish smile on Cathy's face and even David is splashing away furiously.

WORKING WITH BUBBLES

Four bubbles and four kicking boards should already be on the side of the pool, so put the bubble on Adam and Beth, give a bubble to Cathy to play with, and this time just look through David as if he is not there. All this should take place on the shallow side of the pool where the children can comfortably stand, or even sit.

Take Adam by the hand, walking in front of him, and gently pull him along to the three-foot six-inch depth. Here the water comes to your waist but is above the children's heads. Ask Adam to show you if he can kick his legs, which of course he can. Tell him that he is going to learn to swim like a doggie, which will appeal to him very much. If he has a dog at home, ask what the dog's name is and for the rest of the lesson don't call him Adam, but say, "Come, Rover, let's go for a swim."

Do the same with Beth, and when it's Cathy's turn, don't put the bubble on her yet, but hold her, not by the hand, but under the shoulder. Do two or three rounds with the children before you turn to David, who, in the meantime, has quieted down, wondering what's going to happen to him, and watching the other children having their turns. Without warning, pick David up under the shoulders and take him along. He will start crying again but the minute you put him back down in the shallow part he will be quiet.

Gradually start moving the children's hands under the water in a circular movement. Halfway through the lesson, put the bubble on Cathy, who by this time is willing to do anything, especially after seeing that the other children have come to no harm.

With David, just play it by ear. If he calms down enough to have the bubble on, put it on by all means, but don't force the issue. David might carry on for another two or three lessons, but once he settles down or becomes what I call broken in, you will find that he is going to be the quickest to learn of the four.

The reason for all the tantrums is not that he doesn't like the water (mother tells me that in the bathroom he can hold his head under for a long time), but because he strongly objects to a stranger ordering him about. Very likely, he has not started kindergarten yet and this swimming lesson is his first encounter with the big, cruel world that exists outside his home.

Having the bubble on tends to make the children kick in an odd way. Instead of making a splash on the top of the water they will bend their knees in under their tummies like riding a bicycle or running. There is a reason for this. Not being able to relax, they curl up. You know yourself that if you have a cramp or a stomachache, the most comfortable position is to draw the knees up to the stomach. These children are having a new experience in a strange element—water—so naturally, at first, they are frightened and fight their natural buoyancy. Once they relax, their feet will float up.

Wearing the bubble doesn't help much because the bubble is a big, bulky lump on their backs. Those children who have spent considerable time in the water and, more important, are willing to put their faces in the water, will be the ones whose legs will float naturally. After they take a few turns across the pool and back, kicking their legs and moving their arms under the water, with your help, of course, it's time to put them on a kicking board, still wearing the bubble.

Why Use a Bubble at All?

To start a three-year-old swimming takes much longer before he can swim on his own than if you use the bubble. It just makes things much easier. Normally, a child would first have to learn to float, but this stage can be bypassed by attaching a bubble. In this way you have a child swimming on his own in four or five lessons. For a child who hasn't yet learned how to put his face into the water, swimming around, even though supported by a bubble, gives him great freedom, and very early on he can feel he has achieved something.

When I was young, before my competitive swimming years, my mother, like many mothers, decided I should learn to play the piano. So the boring lessons began. To this day, I remember the frustration of not being able to play a little sonata immediately. Needless to say, after six months of taking lessons, I still couldn't play a single tune. Those little three-year-olds have the same frustration by not being able to swim immediately. Using the bubble as a teaching aid sets them free. The more they swim with it, the more they gain confidence and strength. For those who have a swimming pool at home, this can be a great help. But remember: Constantly remind your child that he can only swim with his bubble on. After a while, children will understand, and won't dream of going into the water without it.

As a teacher, you should experiment with all swimming aids before attempting to use them. This is especially true of the bubble. Strap it on your body and pretend you are a three-year-old frightened child who might cry just by having water splashed in his face. You can feel that the buoyancy of the bubble is reassuring. Next, pretend that you are dog paddling with your feet splashing out of the water, but you are still wary of getting your face totally wet. As your body is higher in the water, you will feel less lift from the bubble. Finally, float and swim with your face in the water as all your pupils will eventually do. You will see that because your body is horizontal and high in the water you will not even feel you are wearing the bubble. When your pupil achieves this stage and the bubble is riding out of the water, there is no longer a need for it.

At the end of each lesson make sure that the bubble is taken off for a short while and make the child do something without it. Find out what he likes to do best, whether kicking on the board, floating on the back, or whatever, and do that particular exercise with him, *without* the bubble. It's a good idea to take the bubble off for playtime (unless the swimming pool hasn't a shallow end).

USING THE KICKING BOARD

Place their hands on each side of the board with their thumbs on the upper side. Make sure that their arms are always stretched out, the chin down in the water. On the first round, put your hands over the child's hands. This gives support and helps to pull the child along. If he tends to pull the board in toward his tummy, let the board go with one hand and keep pressing his chest back with the other, so that eventually he will hold his arms straight again.

As you are walking backwards, keep talking to him to take his mind off what he is doing, and slowly work your hands back until you are just holding the end of the board that is nearest to you. Slowly let the board go altogether and say, "Isn't that lovely? The water holds you up and I'm not even helping." Depending on the child, what follows is either an angelic smile or a desperate "Please hold on to me!" Let him have his way. In the first two or three lessons, it is better to follow the child's instincts, as this is the time when he has to learn to trust you. I always make a point of telling the child beforehand, "I'm going to let you go now."

There will be children who will just float aimlessly around—usually the younger ones. It takes a while for them to realize that if they want to move from point A to B, they have to kick their legs to get there. By the

end of the first lesson, though, all the children should be kicking around with their kicking boards.

As you are introducing new things like dog paddling, kicking, blowing bubbles, holding air, floating, floating on the back, tell the children each time what they are doing. This way they learn the name of each exercise, and after a while, if you say, "Let's do some floating on the back," they turn around all by themselves and lean back into your waiting hands.

DOG PADDLING

After they have learned how to kick on the kicking board, the teacher should go back to the dog paddling. Holding one child's hands firmly, say, "Let this hand go and try to move it all by yourself." She's going to move it in a circular movement as you showed them before. Put your free hand out, and hold her other hand, and this time shake the first hand free. After a few rounds she will change hands quite freely and willingly. If she is kicking her legs steadily while this is going on, without warning shake both of her hands free of yours and let her go on her own.

She will ordinarily either start swimming, holding her head clear above the water, kicking her legs in the bicycle fashion, moving her hands under the water; or she will start yelling at the top of her voice, "Don't let me go!" Or she could keep kicking but lose her balance by putting her face in the water, in which case pick her up immediately, or she will just freeze on the spot—forgetting to kick her legs. If she does this, she is not ready for free swimming, so back to the kicking board and the one-arm swimming.

This kind of free paddling can deceive some parents. They say, "Wow, my child can swim." Unfortunately, this is far from the truth. If you took the bubble off, these children, at this stage, would sink like a stone. Children are free and safe swimmers only if they can swim in a horizontal position, head under the water and coming up for air.

BLOWING BUBBLES AND TAKING A BIG BREATH

When teaching a child to swim, you must remember that it is equally important for the child to learn how to blow bubbles as it is to hold the breath. When the body is floating horizontally, the reason it stays up is the lungs are full of air, and that gives the body buoyancy. After teaching hundreds of adults to swim, I have come to realize that when I ask my pupils to take a big breath, there was some kind of communication problem, because the result never satisfied me. Taking a big breath for a nonswimmer is different from taking a big breath for a swimmer. The best way to describe how to take a breath as a swimmer is to imagine you have a cold and your breathing is stuffed up. You put a towel over your head, and deeply inhale steam and medication through your mouth. This is the kind of deep breathing, through the mouth, that is used in swimming. The blowing out has to be equally forceful and through the mouth. If water goes into your nose, it's because by mistake you are partially breathing through the nose, rather than just the mouth. It's just like sucking a drink through a straw.

Ask your pupil if he can blow a bubble. If he says no, tell him, "Pretend you are blowing out your birthday candles." Many times I sing "Happy Birthday to You" as accompaniment to this effort. Another way is to take his hand and blow hard onto his wet skin. From this he will feel the air on his hand and will know what "blow" means. Still another way for him to feel the impact of the air coming through the water is to put your hands cupped underneath his mouth so that when he blows he can see it, hear it, and feel it.

For some strange reason, when I say to a child, "Close your mouth," it immediately opens up. To overcome this, I have found if I put my fingers on his mouth and say, "Mmmm Mmmm Mmmm Mmmm," it works every time.

When you want him to put his face in the water and hold his breath, you say, *every time*, "Take a big breath, close your mouth, Mmmm Mmmm Mmmm Mmmm. I'm going to count to five." Not only do you have to repeat the instructions every single time, but when saying "Take a big breath," you yourself should take an enormous breath as well.

Don't ask the impossible. If you are just starting off with three seconds under the water and you know the child can hardly do it, don't say, "Now that you have held it for three, let's try and make it ten." (Remember, when the head is under the water, sounds from above can still be heard.)

When the child is holding his breath, insist on his eyes and ears being under the water. It is too early, at this stage, to ask him to open his eyes under the water. This will come later. If you are having difficulty in getting his head under the water during the lesson, this is where helpful parents come in.

Here are a few methods that can be practiced with parent supervision at home:

1. Face in the bathtub water, holding his breath up to the count of five or more.
2. Blowing bubbles at regular intervals.
3. Opening his eyes under the water. Show him colored objects under the water.
4. Alternate between having a shower and a bath. The shower shouldn't be full on, but insist on the child being right underneath. Give her plastic bottles to fill, have her wash dolly's hair under the shower, or let her engage in other play activities.

LEARNING TO FLOAT

Once a child can hold his breath without trouble, without effort, he is ready to learn to float. I never use the expression "deadman's float," as it has a sinister sound to it. Can you imagine a bright kid asking, "What's a deadman's float?" Then you will have to say, "That's how you float when you drown and you are dead."

If the water is shallow, a good method is to have the children kneel down with their arms outstretched, take a deep breath, and gently fall forward. Or, if the water is above their head, stand facing them and hold their arms, making sure that their legs are outstretched and that they are lying on their tummy flat on top of the water. The first time you do that, tell the child, "I want you to take a deep breath and put your face in the water. I'm going to count to five and will let you go while you are under the water, and when you run out of breath I'm going to fish you out."

By this time the relationship between the teacher and pupil should be so good that the child will know that he can trust the teacher, and that if she says, "I will fish you out," she really means it. The best way to do this is to have the child touch your shoulders while your free hands are supporting his hips. At the word "Go," he goes under, lets your shoulders go a couple of inches, and for a few short seconds he feels the sensation of floating for the first time in his life.

If it goes without a hitch, praise him profusely. Repeat this a few times, then let him stand in the shallow part of the pool if there is one while you stand back in the deeper part, at first just a few feet away. Hold your arms out, ready to catch him, and say, "You try to float here to me." As time goes on, you can increase the distance between you and the child.

LEARNING TO SWIM

The next step is to get them paddling with their faces in the water. This should be done without their bubbles on, which is a bit of a drawback initially because they are used to having them on their backs. At the start they will still tend to kick their legs downward.

Tell them to take a deep breath, face in the water, and move their arms in a circular movement while kicking their legs. Walk backwards away from them; as you do so, you create a vacuum in front of you. The quicker you walk the stronger the vacuum will be. The children are sucked into it and it gives them a much greater speed than if they swam entirely on their own.

When you feel they need to come up for air, lift their head above the water by putting a hand under their chin. After taking a breath they should go down again. Keep repeating this until they get used to the

idea. With this age group, I still don't insist on blowing bubbles out or holding their breath. Some will blow their breath out, whereas some will hold on to their breath, so that when they come up to the surface they will let the air out before inhaling again. This is the time when a teacher needs to have ten arms instead of two. There are so many faults to correct, it is much better to make corrections by touch rather than lengthy verbal instructions.

If their legs are trailing too low, lift them up a bit by pushing their hips in. If they tend to splash out with their arms, push the arms down. If they forget to come up for air, give a little tap on the top of the head or lift the chin up. Gently correct and nudge them as required.

Some children get a little too game at this stage, so, as you are taking one child at a time, keep looking back at the other three. If one child keeps on jumping into the deep end and has difficulty in getting back to the shallow part, put a bubble back on as a safety measure and then take the bubble off when he is getting personal instruction from you.

Please don't discourage the children from having little tryouts on their own. Don't ridicule them if they can't get back on their own to the edge of the pool. Just walk over nonchalantly and lift them up without saying a word.

OPENING THEIR EYES UNDERWATER

At this stage they are ready to learn how to open their eyes under the water. While they're floating facedown you can say, "Try to open your eyes under the water and see if you can see my swimming suit." They come up very excitedly and say, "I saw your suit, it's black and white." After this you can have a little game with all four children sitting on the side. Say, "I'm going to show you my fingers under the water and you tell me how many fingers you see." Get the brightest child to have a go first, and when he puts his face in (holding his breath), put your outstretched fingers right under his face. Depending on the children's age, show one or two fingers (for the young ones), and three to five (for the older ones).

If you have very young children who can't recognize numbers or even colors, get two different-colored plastic discs, or, for that matter, any similar object, in your hands and say, "I'm going to show you this [red] or that [blue]." The little ones go under the water, have a look and they will point and will say, "I saw that [blue]."

Another good way of getting them to open their eyes is for both teacher and pupil to go under the water together and look into each other's eyes. After a while you can make funny faces at each other, which is tremendous fun.

STAYING UNDER THE WATER

After they learn to float, the teacher should pick one child at a time and, facing him and holding him under the shoulders, push him down vertically under the water. Make sure he is holding his breath. You have to know how long each individual child in your class can stay under the water. Once the child is deep down, gently let the grip go and let him come up on his own. This is the way to learn how to swim in deep water.

Don't forget that a depth of three feet six inches, where an adult can comfortably stand, is as deep to a three-year-old child as six feet six inches is to an adult. By the same token, if a three-year-old has learned and can swim in a three-foot six-inch pool, you can easily let him swim in a six-foot six-inch depth or in a bottomless lake. Deep water is deep water, and once you have learned to swim in it, it doesn't matter where you do it or how deep it is.

Once they can sit on the bottom of the pool, holding their breath, then they can learn to let some air out to blow a bubble. Hold them by the shoulders, push them under the water, and have them blow all the air out; then lift their heads out, having them take a big breath, and push them under the water again. If they tend to touch their eyes with their hands or shake their heads, when they come up out of the water, hold their hands firmly so they can't. Push them up and down in a regular rhythmic movement. Nobody should be allowed to swim with their eyes shut. Without seeing, you lose your balance and sense of direction— and when you swim, you can't afford that. Imagine crossing a busy street with your eyes shut!

KICKING ON THE BACK

To teach the three- to five-year age group floating and kicking on their backs, the same method should be employed as teaching the babies. Teach them to float first, standing behind them, supporting their head in one hand, correcting the body position by touch until they float, completely horizontal and relaxed. The teacher should walk backwards and pull the child along in the vacuum she has created. The child's

kicking shouldn't be too powerful, get the balance and movement by moving the arms under the water. I usually say, "Wave to the fishies." Some will take their hands out of the water, at which point you must remind them "Hey, remember, the fish swim under the water." Once this is learned, the teacher can show the class how to turn from kicking on the back to dog paddling and from dog paddling to kicking on the back.

I have given this maneuver a name: "barbecuing a chicken." Children have great imagination and they love turning and turning until they get dizzy. It may sound strange, but when I teach adults to swim, I always aim for them to accomplish this maneuver of being able to change body positions from front to back. To be able to do this in deep water is of great benefit because they know if they tire, or get into breathing difficulty, they can turn on their back and rest.

JUMPING AND DIVING

The children should be introduced to jumping into the water almost as soon as they start to learn to swim. I like them to know what it feels like, as soon as possible, to be able to go under the water and come up again. This way, in every imaginable emergency situation (falling, slipping, being pushed), they will land with their feet first.

Another great advantage of teaching them how to jump into the water is that the thrill of the jumping sensation counterbalances the fear of putting their faces in the water.

Sit the children on the edge of the pool, have them stretch their arms out, and at the word "Go" gently pull them into the water. On the very first attempt the teacher shouldn't let their hands go because she will have to help them find their balance as they come up to the surface.

Now make them stand on the edge of the pool and repeat the same procedure by pulling them in by the hand. After a couple of goes, stand back two steps and try to make them do it on their own. The brave ones will jump as if they had been doing it all their lives. But the not-so-brave will look at you with pleading eyes that seem to say, "What are you trying to do to me? Teacher, come a bit closer."

"No, you try to do it alone. When you get into the water I will fish you out."

"But I can't do it. I'm scared!"

"When I say, 'Ready . . . go,' you jump."

"I caaaaan't!"

This can go on for five minutes, with the poor child deciding he will do it, then at the last moment changing his mind. It's worth waiting for the Big Moment. The decision has to come from the child, so it is not much good giving him a pull or a shove. Needless to say, after that first jump he will turn around and do it again, and again, and again. If the child is not advanced enough, the jumping, and later on the diving, can be done with the bubble.

To teach the children to dive, line them up at the edge of the pool. Make sure their feet are slightly apart, the toes curling onto the very edge of the pool, knees bent. Their arms should be stretched up above their heads, which should be tucked down.

For the first dive, the teacher should stand beside the child and place one hand on his head (holding it down) and her other hand on his bottom. With a

powerful movement, "ease" them into the water. For the second attempt, the teacher should ask the children if they want some help or if they want to do it on their own. Some will say, "I can do it," and some will sheepishly look at you and say, "Yes, please, help me."

The difference in individual style is amazing. Some will do a belly flop, some will start off as if they are going to dive but halfway through the air change to a jump. And then, occasionally, some will perform a perfect swallow dive. At this age the teacher shouldn't correct the clumsy divers. Let them do what they feel like doing. There is plenty of time for improving technique later on.

Jumping and diving without a bubble on is only advisable when children can swim at least five or six yards on their own. Once children have started diving, they will want to do it forever and they will do it when you are not watching, so it is better to make sure they can swim on their own to the edge of the pool. At this age of three to five years, the teacher must remind them again and again how important it is to always be sure that the water is deep enough before they jump or dive.

GOING STALE AND OTHER PROBLEMS

How quickly a child is progressing at this stage depends not on how many lessons he receives but on how much supervised playtime he gets. I know from personal experience that children can stagnate at this stage (they can swim with the teacher's assistance but not by themselves), but if the family happens to go away for a two-week vacation where the children spend a considerable time in the water, they come back strong and independent swimmers.

In the three- to five-year age group, it can also happen that children simply do not improve at all. They have reached a plateau and cannot progress any further until they physically grow and develop. In these cases it doesn't do any harm for them to stop having lessons for a while. Take a six-month break. When these children come back again, they are six months older, they have grown stronger, and their ability to learn has improved. Once you have learned something in the water you never forget it, so they can take six months off and pick up where they left off.

When children can swim about six to ten yards on their own, you should stay out of the water for one lesson—pretend that you have a sore tummy or a cold. You should, however, still be in a bathing suit and be sitting on the edge of the pool. Ask the children to go through their paces—blowing bubbles as well as holding their breath, kicking on the board, and then dog paddling a given distance.

Some children will refuse to swim without the teacher being right there in the water with them. This is disappointing for both the teacher and the parents, but the teacher should be firm and make the child swim on his own for a little distance, even if it means that he has to be gently shoved into the water. The child has to learn to be independent. He might cry, but you must insist. The trouble is that young children get so used to the teacher, they have put so much trust in him, that they simply cannot imagine doing things without him being right there within grabbing distance.

Children also tend to feel more secure in the particular swimming pool where they first learned to swim. This too can be a problem. I have known children to drag their parents as far as ten miles to the swimming pool where they first learned to swim, rather than going nearby to a similar-size pool and surroundings. If a child is too attached to the teacher and swimming pool, the parents should make a trip to another swimming pool and demonstrate to the child that he can swim anywhere.

How often I have heard from desperate parents after a weekend outing, "He wouldn't do a thing for us." This, of course, happens quite often, but parents have to persevere and make their children do what they know they are capable of doing. Of course I am not advocating that children be thrown into the pool. To throw a nonswimmer into the water is terrible. One child out of ten will probably swim out quite unharmed, but the other nine will have such a fright that they may never get rid of their fear. However, I do insist on making children do what they have been taught—no more, and no less. If one child had twenty lessons and can swim and jump in my pool, I would certainly expect him to show mummy and daddy how he can float.

5
FIVE-TO TEN-YEAR-OLDS— ADVANCED SWIMMING

Now it is time to teach the five- to ten-year-olds an efficient freestyle. The following teaching method could be used with a three- or four-year-old (and adults too!), provided he or she is already familiar and comfortable with the water. One cannot bypass stages, so when one has learned to float and dog paddle, it is time to learn freestyle.

At this point, I am assuming that when the children come for their swimming lesson they can already float and thrash along in some fashion. The chapter heading may be misleading. It does not, in any way, mean that if a child has turned five he should immediately be taught freestyle.

To start off, children have to learn how to push and glide. By *push,* I mean with slightly bent knees giving yourself a gentle spring forward. By *glide,* I mean holding your breath (Mmmm, Mmmm) and floating toward the instructor. The teacher should stand back from the children a couple of yards and say, "Arms up, take a deep breath, and glide over to me." After that, they can do push-and-glide with kicking. When they are not facing the teacher, they should be instructed to stand back from the wall and practice going toward it. When the teacher wants to increase the distance, she should move back one step at a time, or tell the children to stand further away from the wall. It is not a good idea to stand them against the wall and say, "Kick as far as you can go," because when children know exactly how far they are expected to go, they make a great effort to get there, but if they are allowed to stop anywhere they will give up more easily.

MOVING THEIR ARMS

Before commencing the arm movements, the teacher should demonstrate how to move one arm in a circle. When demonstrating, hold the arm stiffly straight, horizontally and in front, fingers pointed, palms down. Swing the arm down to the leg, sweep it back behind as far as it will go, then bring the arm up and over slowly without bending the elbow. Children should do this standing out of the water, moving one arm first, then the other. When they are moving their arms correctly, holding them straight, they can practice moving them continuously.

Why Should the Arms Be Straight?

The correct freestyle stroke is done by bending the elbows slightly over the water with the tips of the fingers touching the water first, followed by the firm but bent wrist. My many years of teaching experience, however, have taught me that if one shows a child a slightly bent elbow they will overemphasize the movement. Their arms enter the water at too sharp an angle, about 45 degrees, which cuts the freestyle stroke in half. By showing a straight-arm entry, they get the feeling of stretching out in front, reaching down into the water, and thus achieving an economical stroke technique. As they are progressing they loosen up and, without anybody telling them, they begin to bend their arms naturally, so that they finish up swimming a relaxed and correct freestyle stroke. If a child, by some miracle, looks as if he is going to do this, for goodness' sake don't tell him to keep his arms straight (but, believe me, this doesn't happen often.)

After showing them how to move their arms, tell them, "Take a deep breath, put your face in the water, and swim *slowly* to me, moving your arms." Have them do this a few times before you start correcting them. Look under the water and watch their arms and how they pull.

If the child doesn't pull down on the center line of his body, correct this by showing him the angle he is using, then show him the correct angle. Tell him to open his eyes under the water and watch his hands going down. He can see for himself what you are talking about—whether his arms are going down straight or slipping out to the side. The teacher can say, "If you pull out to the side, you are pushing the water away from you, but if you pull your arms straight down, you will push the water underneath you." (By the way, it's not true that the fingers should be pressed tightly against one another and that it is a capital sin to have the fingers open.) Watch carefully that nobody swims with a bent elbow.

BREATHING

When doing freestyle you turn your head to the side out of the water to breathe. Breathing correctly is a major element in swimming successfully. Later in life many people would like to enjoy swimming for recreation but they cannot do so because their breathing is not coordinated properly. The side you breathe on is determined by whether you are right- or left-handed. Right-handed people find it easier to turn their head to the right side, left-handed people find it easier to turn to the left.

Get a waterproof permanent marker and paint a dot on the child's hand after asking which hand he holds his pencil in at school. As you put the dot on declare that this, from now on, is going to be his *breathing arm*. If a child is too small to know which hand he holds his pencil in, the surest way to find out whether he or she is right- or left-handed is to ask the mother.

Never talk about right or left, just call the spotted hand the "breathing arm," and the plain one the "pushing arm." Keep putting the spot on until such time that when you ask the child, "Which is your breathing arm?" he automatically lifts it up. Using the marker helps greatly because after they go home from their swimming lesson, they carry the dot on their hands for hours, reminding them all the time, "This is my breathing arm." You will find that the younger they are, the more proudly they wear this mark.

When explaining for the first time, have the children come out of the water and show them individually what you want them to do. "When your breathing arm comes out of the water, you turn your head back, looking at your breathing arm, and take a b-i-i-i-g breath. When your breathing arm goes into the water, you put your head back in the water too and blow b-i-i-i-g bubbles." As you explain this, stand behind each child, holding the breathing arm in your right hand while the left hand is on the top of the child's head. This way you can synchronize the head movements with the arms.

Keep telling them to look back on their breathing arm, putting their chin on their shoulder as they breathe in; then, let the head come up, and roll the chin down to the chest as they blow out.

When teaching outdoors, it's a good idea to let the children do this land drill before they enter the water, otherwise you might have four shivering children unable to give their attention because they are cold.

If the children are tall enough to stand up comfortably in the three-foot six-inch end of the pool, have them walk a certain distance in the pool, practicing the above-mentioned drill, but this time have them put their faces into the water to blow the bubbles. This walking is a good way of getting them to coordinate their movements, because if they make a mistake they can hear your instruction to correct it more easily than if they were already swimming. The mistakes they make while walking like this—bending their arms, not lifting their pushing arm when blowing out, jerking their head up, holding on to their breath, and so forth—they will also do when swimming. So it's important to spot and then correct these mistakes before they start swimming.

If the pool has a fair amount of shallow space in it, they can do a "crocodile walk": with both hands touching the bottom of the pool, and their legs stretched out completely, they can start walking on their hands. As the breathing arm comes out, they turn their heads back and take a big breath. When the pushing arm comes out, they blow out a big bubble.

When you think of it, turning the head to one particular side only can be a very confusing matter. What you look at changes. For example, when you are swimming down the length of the pool you keep breathing toward the fence. But when you come back you are not looking at the fence, but at the house. If you have the mark on your hand it makes it easier to tell when you should be looking at the fence and when at the house.

When the children have a fair idea of how and when to turn their heads, and when to breathe in and out, the teacher should stand in front of each child and make him swim a short distance.

FAULTS TO WATCH FOR AND HOW TO CORRECT THEM

Too Much Kicking

Too much kicking will thrust the body forward, using up too much oxygen and energy in the process and interfering with the arms going slowly around in a relaxed way. The secret of breathing well is to do it slowly, allowing time for the lungs to expand and contract. Very often the child will move his arms too fast because he is kicking too fast. To correct this, instruct the child to swim without kicking his legs. You will notice that his arm stroking will become more relaxed. Although he thinks that he's not kicking and is just dragging his feet behind, you will happily notice that his six-beat kick has slowed down to a two-beat kick.

Not Enough Kicking

Some children seem as if they are only dragging their feet, and when put on a kicking board, they don't seem to be able to move at all. They are probably kicking from the knees, instead of the hips.

Some children have enormous chests and very strong arms. When they swim, they propel themselves through the water using their arms only. There are famous swimmers who have highly irregular styles. Instead of using what's considered a normal six-beat kick, they use an "abnormal" combination of a two-beat and a four-beat kick. (A six-beat kick is six kicks to one complete arm circle.) These swimmers usually have a strong upper body and use their legs only as a balance to their powerful arm stroke.

Every action has a reaction. If you pick up a heavy bucketful of water and carry it a certain distance, the other arm will automatically spring up as a balance. In swimming, kicking serves as a balance to breathing. When the swimmer turns even slightly for air, his body loses its balance because of the change of position, so the opposite leg will kick out slightly more.

I remember having a pupil called Matthew who came to my swimming school for style correction. He was swimming a very pretty stroke, having spent the previous four or five years in his own backyard pool. Matthew had taken up swimming as a sport and spent the summer training every day with me at an outdoor, Olympic-size pool. Halfway through the season, Matthew's father came to me and, horrified, he showed me how his son's pretty six-beat kick turned into an ugly two-beat kick. I explained to him that doing two to three miles in a practice session had built up his upper body. When not flat out, he used the two-beat kick, but in sprints, his kicking speed increased to six beats.

When children are not kicking a lot, don't be alarmed. If they are swimming along, moving at a reasonable speed, give them plenty of kicking-board work. With practice they will eventually get the knack of kicking.

Holding the Breath

Until somebody has mastered the breathing technique, it's definitely easier to swim along just holding on to your breath and not letting it out. The trouble is that sooner or later you have to stop.

Some children will look as if they are breathing in and out; they open their mouths when turning their heads to the side and at the right time they roll their heads back into the water. Children are very good actors and imitators, but the teacher with a sharp eye will be able to see if the child *really* lets the air out. If

he is breathing out properly you will see the bubbles. If the pool where you are teaching is not a long one, say thirty or forty feet long, a child might even swim from one end to the other and appear to be breathing properly, when in fact he is not.

To correct this particular breathing fault, the teacher should have the child do an exercise called "one-arm breathing." One arm is placed on the top of a kicking board, leaving the other, the breathing arm, to move alone. Say, "Turn your head, look back when you're breathing out, take a b-i-i-i-g breath, and as your breathing arm goes into the water, blow a b-i-i-i-g bubble out." If necessary, have the child do this for a couple of lessons.

Alternatively, the child should do a lot of kicking on the kicking board, holding on to it with both hands, lifting the head up but not too far out of the water, taking a big breath, then blowing a bubble into the water. When coming up for air, the child should leave his chin on the water, and when blowing out make sure that his ears are well and truly under the water. If a child is very young and can't understand what you are saying, place your hand under his mouth as he blows out so he can feel the impact of the air hitting the hand. Praise him when you feel the bubbles.

Stopping After Three Strokes

Your prize pupil suddenly develops a bad habit of stopping after three strokes. You look at him from the right side and you look at him from the left side. You climb out of the water to see if you can pick a fault from there; you ask him if he feels all right, has he got a tummy ache; and then in desperation you throw your arms up: "I can't find any fault in him! Why on earth does he stop after every three strokes?"

There is nothing wrong with him—he's lazy! If the teaching takes place in a shallow pool, where he can touch bottom, he will find the easy way out and put his foot down the minute he feels tired. If the swimming pool has a deep water area, transfer him there immediately and continue the lessons there for a while. In the deep water his style will suffer a bit, but at least he will swim from one end of the pool to the other.

Left Arm Dragging

So much attention is given to the vital coordination of breathing and the breathing-arm stroke, that it is no wonder the other arm becomes neglected.

Right-handed children who find it hard to master the breathing will probably be rolling too much on their left side and therefore will hardly be using the left arm, the pushing arm, at all. In bad cases, they may even roll onto their backs. There is a tendency in everybody to use one arm and one leg more than the other. If the fault is not too bad, leave it alone for a while, and go back to correcting it once the breathing has been mastered. In the next chapter I will deal with bilateral breathing, which is an absolutely marvelous way to get rid of this lopsidedness.

In the early learning stages there is one good method that can be used to get the pushing arm moving. Put the breathing arm on top of the kicking board, and only move around the pushing arm, but this time have it so the head *does not go into the water*. Make sure that the child lifts his pushing arm very high and that, on entry, it goes straight down and does not pull out on the side.

Lifting the Head Out of the Water

This is one fault that everybody has in the early learning stages. The child rolls his head and looks back at his breathing arm but, instead of keeping his chin down to finish blowing out, at the last moment he jerks his head out in front. This is very bad.

The swimmer's body should be in a flat position, and if the head lifts up out of the water the balance will be gone. Like a seesaw, the minute the head comes up, the feet will have to come down. Very often the reason for the head popping out in front, instead of being turned to the side, is that the children swim with their eyes closed. When the eyes are closed you cannot see where you are going. Instead of opening the eyes under the water, they only open their eyes when they breathe in. While they have their eyes open, they swing their heads up and forward to see where they are going.

Asthmatic children hate the feeling of their faces being under the water. They have a claustrobophic sensation and are prone to panic, fearing they won't be able to lift their head out of the water in time to take another breath.

To correct the lifting of the head out front, the children should do a lot of the crocodile walk, the teacher walking along beside them, guiding the head movement with her hands. Also, one-arm breathing can be practiced, making sure that the chin touches the shoulders, then rolls down to the chest and back again.

Can't Get Rid of the Air

I often hear it from my adult pupils: "When I put my face into the water, I somehow can't get rid of the air."

This can happen to children too. The time allowed between strokes is just not long enough to get rid of the air. In these cases, it's advisable to teach breathing on every four strokes.

For the normal freestyle, you take a breath every time the breathing arm comes out of the water, and you blow out when the pushing arm goes over. Breathing on every fourth stroke means that you take a breath when the breathing arm comes out and you hold it for the next three strokes. The counting starts when an arm reaches out in front, so it goes: Take a breath—that's one, face in the water—two, three, four—then take a breath again, face in the water; two, three, four.

There are two ways of getting rid of the air for this four-stroke style:

1. Let the air out slowly, bit by bit, carefully economizing to make it last through the four strokes.
2. Hold on to it until the very last stroke, and let it out with a big blow, and then take a breath in the normal way.

When first introducing breathing on every fourth stroke, it is advisable to let the pupils walk in shoulder-deep water, practicing breathing on every four strokes. This way everybody can experiment to find out which of the two methods of breathing suits them best.

Doing Freestyle with a Little Bit of Dog Paddling

Many children are not strong enough to swim correct freestyle immediately. They will roll their heads to their breathing arm, they will bring their arms straight out of the water, and they won't jerk their heads up in front, but, as they are pulling their breathing arm under the water, getting ready to take a breath, they will do two little dog paddles and then continue to stroke.

As they get stronger, they will drop the habit; if it worries the teacher or parent, a child could have a bubble on again for a while. With the bubble on, they can relax and won't have to struggle to do the correct stroke.

Not Strong Enough

Your pupil swims correctly but when you tell him to increase his distance, his beautiful and freshly learned style greatly suffers. In cases like this, regardless of age, I put my smallest bubble on them. The bubble gives the necessary lift, so instead of struggling to stay on top, they can concentrate more on swimming "pretty"! This way, there is less chance of developing bad swimming habits. As with the beginning swimmers, swimming with the bubble on increases their strength, and when the time comes, the bubble can be easily discarded.

Ugly Style

The swimmer's style is not pretty; in fact, the style is ghastly! The child looks as if he has ten arms, twenty legs, and at least five heads. He doesn't know what to do, splashes wildly, but somehow manages to beat all the other children in a swimming race.

The teacher should try to analyze if there is anything technically wrong with him, but if there isn't, just leave him alone. With more practice, it is likely that he will smooth out his bad habits.

On the other hand, he could be an ugly swimmer for the rest of his life. Many of the world's great swimmers have had ugly styles yet their performances were certainly not. So don't let it worry you, provided the technique is sound.

SWIMMING DRILLS

With Kicking Board:
> Kicking.
> Kicking, blowing bubbles, lifting the head vertically.
> Kicking, blowing bubbles, turning the head to the side.
> One-arm breathing.
> Putting the breathing hand on the board and moving the pushing arm only.

Without Kicking Board:
> Crocodile walk.
> Walking in shoulder-deep water.
> Breathing and bubbling.
> Swimming with flippers on.
> Swimming with bubble on.

Land Drills:
> Practicing arm movement and coordination of arms and breathing.

DEEP-WATER TREATMENT

Many children will jump into deep water without bothering much about the consequences. They will either panic or just swim out. The majority of them have to be carefully guided into the art of treading water.

When children are taken for the first time into the deep part of the pool, I proceed as follows. The four children in the class all sit down on the edge of the pool and the teacher eases them, one by one, into the water, each child holding on to the edge of the pool. Once all four are in the water, the teacher gives the command for them to take a big breath, put their faces in the water, and hold the breath for five to ten seconds.

With each child in turn, the teacher kneels on the side of the pool and, holding him firmly by the hand, pushes him vertically down. The teacher should name each child, saying first, "Come on, John, I'm going to hold on to your hands, I'm not going to let them go, and I will push you down. Make sure *not* to blow any bubbles out and to open your eyes."

After several dunkings, the teacher should encourage the child to do it on his own. By this time he has felt the force that brings him up to the surface of the water, so there shouldn't be much protesting. Some children will still cling to the edge of the pool while they push themselves under, and some of them will have gained enough confidence to let go of the wall. Repeat this dunking a few times, then get the children out of the water and make them sit on the edge.

Taking one at a time, ease them back into the water and ask them to dog paddle or do freestyle (whichever they can do the best) along the wall for about three or four yards. After completing the distance, praise them and comment on how easy it was and how it feels not a lot different from swimming in the shallow pool.

Make the children do this at least five times before you get into the water.

If the teacher is not a strong swimmer, she should find a spot in the swimming pool where she can still comfortably stand, say, four to five feet in depth; for children that depth is still deep. Stand back three to five yards away from the wall and ask one child at a time to swim out to you and back. As they improve, you can ask them to swim around you and then back.

Next, take the group of children over to the deepest part of the swimming pool, and stand them in a line. Now they will have to jump in one by one. In Olympic-size pools, the deepest part is usually six feet six inches, and at the very end of the pool there is usually a ladder. If the deep-water treatment is done in an Olympic pool, take the children down there and do the jumping at the deep-end corner. If it is in a private swimming pool, try to find a similar spot, so that after jumping and coming up they can reach the ladder immediately.

Before proceeding to the big First Jump, warn them that the water is deep, and the first time they jump it will feel as if it takes ages to get to the top of the water again. Add with a cheerful smile that the second jump will be much easier and that jumping into the deep end is really great fun. The children standing there, listening to you, don't believe a word you say; they are not happy at all and, if they had a chance, they would even run back to mummy. But the teacher should try to ignore the desperation on their little faces.

Pick the bravest one of the group and make him do it first. The others will be standing right at the edge, looking down at the water swirl coming up from the child who has just jumped. A little head comes up to the top, grabs the ladder and says, "Boy, that was good!" Repeat the jumping about five times and that should do for their first deep-water lesson.

One time in deep water doesn't qualify a child as fit to swim in deep water all the time. But if a child can swim the width of an Olympic pool, or twenty yards unaccompanied, he can be left more to his own devices. If a child doesn't feel sure of himself, he will not play in deep water, but rather stay in the shallow end of the pool.

If a child has been taught and shown how to jump in deep water, no great harm can come to him. Even if he is not confident enough to play in the deep, should he accidentally fall or be thrown in, he will know how to get up to the top of the water again, having experienced it before.

I know from personal experience that it's hard for a mother to believe that her child, who couldn't swim a stroke two or three weeks before, can now swim and play in deep water. My own little girl, Bobbie, when she was three, simply refused to go near the deep end although by that time she was swimming—rather dog paddling—in the shallow end. One day, some bigger girls took her into the deep end and made her jump in. From then on she never went back to the shallow part, saying, "That was for babies only." Some afternoons when the pool was filled with a capacity crowd, my heart would beat very fast when I saw her little head bobbing up and down among the other swimmers. But I knew she was safe because she could easily swim to the side.

6

COMPETITIVE SWIMMING:

TEACHING THE BUTTERFLY, THE BACKSTROKE, THE BREASTSTROKE, AND THE FREESTYLE

ABOUT COMPETITIVE SWIMMING

There is a lot to be said for competitive swimming and, in the same breath, there is a lot to be said against it.

How Is a Swimmer Born?

One child learns to swim, does so without much effort, and falls in love with it. The parent looks around for organized swimming in their community, for clubs, youth organizations, or some city-sponsored activity. The child attends training sessions, he wins his first race, and from then on there is no way to stop him. He starts to spend more and more time at the swimming pool. Swimming soon becomes a way of life. It is not unusual for a child these days to be in training and competition at the age of six. Starting that early, they will often retire from swimming at the age of fourteen. My daughter retired at age seven.

In my competitive swimming days it was thought that if a child started racing early he would physically wear out. This has been proven wrong. It is hardly possible to overtire a child. At the age of six, he is capable of doing six miles a day (in two training sessions), going to bed at night completely exhausted, and waking in the morning ready to go again. But just as in my daughter's case, they can have psychological burnout—too much, too soon. When I am asked by parents who are thinking of entering their children in competition at an early age, I try to restrain them from entering too early. When possible, I recommend a low-key organization. There is plenty of time for the pressure later on.

The Pros and Cons of Competitive Swimming

In my opinion, the big advantage of competitive swimming is that very early in their lives children learn to be independent as well as learn that, if they want to achieve anything, they have to work for it themselves, with no mother or father to help them. In a way this is a little cruel, but after all, life can be cruel too. A swimmer is a lonely person. Although the squad members are around, the swimmer has got to do the work entirely on her own. Unless there is a driving force behind her to do better and strive for perfection, she is never going to succeed professionally.

Swimmers have different motivations. Some do it for

the pleasure of physical exhaustion, some to prove to themselves that they are capable of achieving something. Others will do it because of the pleasure of winning, some for health reasons, and still others, perhaps wrongly, will do it because their father wants them to.

There are many pleasures in training and competition and there are many disappointments too. Losing an important race can become a tragedy. Social life suffers—there is no time for parties, visiting the zoo, or even holidays. I must say, in fairness, that a social life does exist—but all your friends are fellow swimmers.

I started competitive swimming at eleven years and stopped at eighteen and a half. After the Melbourne Olympic Games, I had achieved everything I wanted. Being a member of an Olympic team, traveling to many countries as a swimming representative, holding twenty or so national titles, leading the top ten in a world list in my particular event, and most exciting of all, being a member of a world-record-breaking relay team. Still, I often think if I was given another chance, would I do it again? I probably would, but I often feel like a social outcast for not being able to play tennis, ride a horse, ski, or play the piano.

Most swimming coaches think becoming a champion is worth all the sacrifices you have to make. But I think competitive swimming is fun only as long as nobody takes it too seriously. When families sacrifice so many years of their lives, giving up all their free time carting children to training sessions and swimming competitions, I think it is a little sad. Certainly there are a few exceptional talents and they should carry on by all means, but I see so many mediocre children involved in competitive swimming who really don't care one way or the other; their main motivation is that their parents get pleasure out of seeing their offspring on the starting block. How often have I seen fathers scolding their children after a badly swum race? Competitive swimming should be between the coach and the pupil, and *nobody else* should be involved.

The reader might ask why, after saying this, am I involved in the swimming game? Well, I love it! I love passing on my knowledge to children, knowing that the gift I'm giving them will last a lifetime. Coaching is a bit like a lottery—occasionally one finds a perfectly talented, intelligent child, and to guide her until she achieves success is a satisfying accomplishment. Equally satisfying is to have a nervous, self-conscious child and, through training and successful competitive swimming, see her blossom into a self-assured, confident individual.

The swimming pool atmosphere is a healthy one, with boys and girls mixing freely. Running around in swimming suits, they don't look on each other as "boy" or "girl," but rather as friends.

Schoolwork, surprisingly, doesn't suffer from all the outside school activities. Children who swim learn to concentrate much better than a nonswimmer, so doing homework takes a half hour of concentrated work compared with two hours for the nonswimmer, who fidgets, plays, and is distracted by TV.

Now to the four competitive strokes.

THE BUTTERFLY

Arm Movements

Standing out of the water, have the children put both of their arms out straight in front of them and push them down to the legs. They should keep pushing back as far as the arms can go. At this point the palms of the hands should be turned upward. With a roll of the shoulders, they should bring their arms over and around, so that they brush past their ears and arrive back at the original position. Repeat this a few times.

Kicking

Back in the water say to them, "Take a deep breath, face in the water, and butterfly across the pool."

One small voice: "Kicking too?"

"No, Gregory, I purposely didn't say anything about kicking; do whatever you like."

So the small group takes off. Two out of the four children will do a natural dolphin kick, one will drag his feet behind and move only his arms, and the other will do freestyle kicking with the butterfly arms. Keep repeating this and don't correct any of the kicking at all, just make sure that the arm stroke resembles the butterfly stroke.

Breathing

There are two ways of breathing for the butterfly. One is to breathe every stroke (remember you always start counting a stroke in the front), and the other is to breathe on every second stroke.

When children are learning, it's easier for them to start off breathing on every second stroke, and when they get stronger and more efficient they can return to breathing on every stroke.

Have the children hang on to the edge of the pool and do some breathing and bubbling, lifting their heads vertically.

"Try to take a quick breath and then try to blow out a very slow long bubble."

First the teacher should demonstrate this, standing out of the pool. Arms stretched out in front, take a breath and bring your head down as if it is going into the water. Keep your head down for the completion of the first stroke; then, still holding your head down, make a complete circle again to finish the second stroke. This sounds highly technical, but in practice it's really easy.

Have the children practice this first standing in shoulder-deep water, then walking along the pool. When the teacher is satisfied that all the children are breathing in at the beginning of the first stroke, she can then ask them to try to do it while they swim. Even at this stage there shouldn't be any correction or advice given on the kicking. This way even a four-year-old can butterfly ten or fifteen yards, doing the correct butterfly arm stroke and breathing without much effort.

WALKING IN PAIRS
To practice breathing and to make it easier, the children could do the following exercise.

Try to select children who are the same size and pair them off, in the pool, one in front of the other, facing the same direction. The one in the front will lift both his legs up, stretch them out, and hold them still. The other child behind grabs the legs and holds on to them like a wheelbarrow, then starts walking forward slowly pushing the "working-horse." The "working-horse" starts butterflying, moving his arms and breathing. At the end of the pool the two should change positions and do the same thing coming back.

Doing the butterfly this way is fun and the children seem to love it. Walking in pairs can be used for breaststroke breathing too.

Dolphin Kicking

Have the children hold on to the edge of the pool, then ask them to try to do a new kind of kicking—dolphin kicking.

Keeping the knees lightly together, the children should move *both* of the legs up and down vertically simultaneously. The legs shouldn't be rigid; the knees can bend slightly, and the hips and upper body can move as well. Once they've got the hang of this, have them turn to face the pool.

"Does anybody know what a dolphin is?"

"It's Flipper on television."

"That's right. How about trying to be Flipper and try to swim just like him."

"But he doesn't do dolphin kicking."

"Of course he does, he's a dolphin. Now, put your hands on the sides of your legs so you don't move your arms, take a deep breath, face in the water, and try to dolphin-kick across the pool. Look like a snake, like a rocking-horse, and like a dolphin, all rolled into one. Don't be afraid to wriggle your bottoms."

So off they go. Surprisingly, they *all* do a perfect dolphin kick.

First have them practice dolphin kicking by holding their hands on their sides. Later on, their arms could be stretched out in front. Practicing dolphin kicking while holding on to a kicking board makes them rather stiff, so try to avoid using it. When their dolphin kicking goes well, put the butterfly arm movements and dolphin kicking together.

I think I should digress to explain how that rather weird combination of butterfly (insect) and dolphin (swimming mammal) came into being.

Once there were only three swimming strokes: freestyle, backstroke, and breaststroke. At the 1952 Helsinki Olympics a Hungarian girl won the 200 meter breaststroke event in incredibly good time using butterfly arm strokes and breaststroke kicking. People using the butterfly arm stroke in a breaststroke race were so much better than those who were doing ordinary breaststroke only that the international swimming body decided to separate the two events. A little bit later on, some swimmers started to experiment with a new kind of kick to combine it with the butterfly. The new kick resembled a dolphin's movements and that's how dolphin kicking was born.

The general public thinks that the butterfly is a hard stroke, but it's not so. To do just a few strokes is very easy. To compete in a butterfly race is another matter. Without training and preparation it would be impossible. But the same goes for all strokes.

I've found that children are eager and willing to learn the butterfly. Maybe it's the romantic name that appeals to them. In a few cases, I had children learning and swimming the butterfly *before* they could do the freestyle.

Anybody who is going to teach the butterfly, please tell the children to watch where the wall is so they don't hit their head. (Cut foreheads have occurred only when the children were doing the butterfly. It somehow doesn't happen with any of the other strokes.)

THE BACKSTROKE

Arm Movements

Standing in the water, the children should move their arms first. They should put one arm out in front so the thumb is facing upward. They should move their arm slowly up and backwards so that, by the time it reaches their ear, the palm of their hand should be turned outward, and when their hand hits the water, their little finger should go into the water first.

Once under the water, they should bring their hand down so that it touches their leg. When lifting it out again, they need to be careful to bring it up very gently so there is not much water dripping off. They should practice one arm first, then the other, and when everything goes well, they should start moving them both, alternating first one and then the other.

Kicking

Before the children start swimming the backstroke, first have them walking backwards in the water, moving their arms. *Don't teach anybody to do backstroke arms unless they can do kicking on the back.*

In the backstroke, the body should be in a very flat position, the ears covered by the water, and the kicking shouldn't be high. The method described here for teaching backstroke is for beginners only. More advanced swimmers bend their arms under the water and the arm pull usually finishes down ten to twelve inches below the level of the hips. I mention the bent arms so that if you see a backstroker bending his arms, causing a little swell, you shouldn't correct it.

The teacher with some knowledge of swimming can teach children to push off on their backs from the wall.

THE BREASTSTROKE

"Has anyone seen a frog jumping or swimming? If you have, that's what the breaststroke looks like."

I have often heard that the breaststroke is so easy, so graceful, so natural, and I say, to teach the correct breaststroke is absolute murder. It's ugly and very unnatural.

The breaststroke used to be pretty and graceful until Americans altered it. It was analyzed, it was photographed, it was dissected, and all movements that were graceful were cut out. The breaststroke was turned into a power stroke.

There is nothing much wrong with the breaststroke itself, but the swimming rules make it very difficult: the arms and legs are not allowed to break the surface of the water; everything has to be symmetrical; after diving in and turning, the swimmer is not allowed to do more than one stroke underwater; at the touch of the wall both hands should touch at the water level. It's easy to teach somebody the breaststroke, that is, a style that resembles the breaststroke. But it's very, very difficult to prepare a child for competition.

Kicking

Before taking children into the water, they have to be shown how the breaststroke kick works. So, have them sit on the floor, balancing on their backside, and draw both their knees up with their heels facing each other

and their toes turned out; now they should straighten their legs out, then bring them together.

Or have them standing, feet turned out, heels facing each other (a bit like first position in ballet). Then they should squat down, turning their knees out and keeping their heels firmly on the floor. While the children are squatting, explain that this is how you want them to hold their legs when they commence the kick.

Another exercise is for them to face and lean on the wall, draw one knee up with feet turned out sideways, then stretch their leg out backwards in a straight line without dropping out of the level, then draw their leg back again to the original position. If the children

repeat this about ten times, they will feel the muscles in their thighs that are needed for breaststroke kicking.

In the water, have them practice breaststroke kicking, holding on to the side of the pool. Make sure that they don't drop a knee and that they keep both of their feet turned out.

Once they've mastered these drills, say to them, "I want you to hold your arms out in front, don't move them, take a deep breath, hold it, and try to breaststroke-kick across the pool."

After a few tries, with their feet only, they can try to move their arms as well.

Arm Movements

Standing in shoulder-deep water facing the pool, their arms should be stretched out in front. They should turn the back of their hands together (like an inside-out praying position), then gently pull sideways, about two inches under the water level. When their arms are out fairly wide, they should bend them from the elbow, gently bringing their arms toward each other, then they should push out in front.

Breathing

Breathing for the breaststroke is similar to that of the butterfly stroke. You can breathe on every stroke or every second stroke. In the early learning stages, I usually tell the children to breathe whenever they feel like it. Some of them will swim holding their heads in for about three or four strokes before they come up for air, and some will come up every stroke.

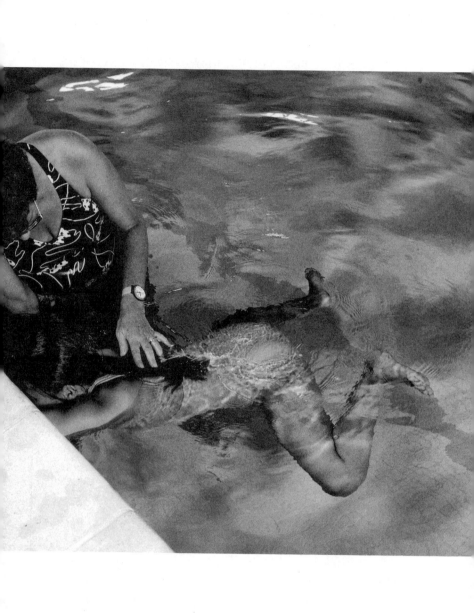

In the advanced stage, swimmers come up for air every stroke. The head should come up for air when the arms are bending halfway through the stroke. The head stays down while the arms go out to the front, glide, and pull back again to the bent-elbow position. The breathing in has to be very quick and the blowing out very slow.

When children learn the breaststroke, they have to spend many hours on the kicking board practicing the kick.

THE FREESTYLE

Freestyle swimming is the most popular stroke, perhaps because it is the fastest form of swimming known to man. The 100 meter freestyle nearly equals the glamour of the 100 meter dash in the Olympics.

The general public is not aware that in swimming competitions from local club level to the Olympics, contestants compete in five types of swimming events. Five? Yes—butterfly, backstroke, breaststroke, freestyle, and the medley, which consists of all four swimming strokes.

All learners should be taught all the strokes. By mastering all, they can specialize in the stroke that suits them best later on. And when in training, it breaks the monotony of the long miles to be able to switch from one stroke to the other. A freestyler, for instance, would gain strength and stamina from doing work on the butterfly. Today, swimming coaches have their pupils do 75 percent of the work in freestyle and the rest is made up of other strokes. Toward main competition they swim more on their individual stroke.

Arm Movements

In the early stages children are taught to swim the freestyle with their arms straight. This way they stretch out in front, reaching deep down and recovering their arms at the very end of the stroke. The more advanced swimmers bring their arms forward slightly bent. The rule is that the elbow should always be higher than the rest of the arm. On entering the water, the wrist should be firm, but not stiff, and the arm should pull along the center line of the body. When under the water, the arm doesn't pull down on a totally straight line, but halfway through the stroke it bends as if the swimmer is writing a big S-shape with his hands.

When correcting a freestyle swimmer's stroke, stand in front of him and watch the entry and the pull from there. If the arm swings out to the side under the water, correct it immediately because it has to stay in the center.

Breathing

There are three types of breathing: breathing on every stroke, breathing on every three (bilateral), and breathing on every four. When the swimmer has to do some long, slow swimming, she could use breathing on every four. If the swimmer swims unevenly, rolls her body, or doesn't lift one arm out as much as the other, she should do her training doing bilateral breathing. When racing a short distance, the swimmer needs a lot of oxygen, so in these cases she breathes on every stroke.

BREATHING ON EVERY STROKE

When the breathing arm comes out of the water, the head is turned back so that the swimmer can take a deep breath. As the breathing arm goes into the water, the head rolls down and starts blowing out. In that time the other arm makes a full circle.

BREATHING ON EVERY THIRD STROKE (BILATERAL)

Here's how to do bilateral breathing: Put the right arm back, take a deep breath, and as the breathing arm goes into the water, start slowly blowing out. Keep the head in the water while the left or pushing arm makes a full circle, as does the breathing arm.

When the pushing arm comes out again, bring the head out of the water, turn to the pushing arm side, take a breath, and put the head in when the pushing arm reaches into the water. Start blowing out and continue to breathe out for the next two strokes.

One—take a breath; two, three—face in the water. One—take a breath on the opposite side; two, three—face in the water.

BREATHING ON EVERY FOURTH STROKE

To breathe on every fourth stroke, do the following:

Put the breathing arm back, take a big breath, and blow it out slowly for the next three strokes. One—take a breath; two, three, four—blow out. One—take a breath; two, three, four—blow out.

In the beginning, children will stop many times, but as time goes on, they will get stronger and stronger and so their distance will increase. If they are used to swimming in deep water, have them to do their training in the middle of the pool and not close to the wall.

Pushing Off the Wall

The more advanced swimmers should learn how to push off from the wall. It's a relatively simple thing to do, but it takes a lot of practice to do it properly. They have to place both of their feet on the wall and push their head under the water before they kick off.

SWIMMING A MILE

Once children have learned to swim fifteen or twenty yards, there is nothing much left to do but to practice. The distance will slowly increase day by day. With proper guidance and swimming once a day for a month, there is no reason why a child shouldn't be able to swim a mile by the end of the month.

The gift of swimming will last a lifetime. Remember, every great swimmer was once a beginner!

*I*NDEX

Accident-avoidance, 17, 19. *See also* Fences
Advanced swimmers (five- to ten-year-olds), 98–116
  laziness in, 108
  swimming drills for, 112
  teaching freestyle stroke to, 98–112
American Academy of Pediatrics, 37
Arm movements
  backstroke, 126
  breaststroke, 131
  butterfly stroke, 121
  freestyle stroke, 99–101, 134
Armbands. *See* Floatie armbands
Asthma, and swimming, 28
Attitude of parent, 17, 19

Babies, young (four months to walking age), 36–68
  classes for, 38–39
  floating lessons, 46–47, 50
  preliminary lessons, 40, 42–43
  reasons for teaching to swim, 36–37
  teaching at home, 40, 42–43, 46–47
  water safety for, 47
Backstroke, 126, 128
Bathing baby, 16–17
Bathtub practice/preparation, 16–17, 19, 37, 53–54
  bubble-blowing, 19, 84–85
Blowing bubbles. *See* Bubble-blowing

Bobbing, 56–57
Breaststroke, 128
  arm movements, 131
  breathing for, 131, 133
  kicking, 130–31
Breathing. *See also* Bubble-blowing; Holding breath
  for breaststroke, 131, 133
  for butterfly stroke, 122–23
  for freestyle stroke, 101–4, 110, 134, 136–37
  practicing, 107, 123
  teaching, 83–85
  water intake, signs of, 65
Bubble floats, 26
  learning freestyle with, 111
  reasons for using, 78–80
  when to stop using, 79
  working with, 76–80
Bubble-blowing, 56, 83–85
  in bathtub, 19, 84–85
Buoys, 23
Butterfly stroke, 121–25
  breathing methods, 122–23
  kicking, 122, 124–25

Cardiopulmonary resuscitation (CPR), learning, 23
Carlile, Forbes, 37, 38
Children. *See* Babies, young; Toddlers to three years; Preschool children (three- to five-year-olds); Advanced swimmers (five- to ten-year-olds)
Classes. *See* Swimming classes
Coaching, 119–20

Competitive swimming, 117–37
  about, 117–20
  pros and cons of, 118–20
Confidence of children
  in self, building, 29
  in teacher, gaining, 72–74,
    85–86
CPR (cardiopulmonary resusci-
    tation), learning, 23
"Crocodile walk," 103
Crying, 34

Deep-water treatment, 113–16
Demonstrating swimming,
    29, 31
Diapers, 24
Disabled children, and swim-
    ming, 28–29
Discipline, importance of, 31–
    32, 34
Diving, teaching, 93, 95. See
    also Jumping into water
Dog paddling, 76–77, 82
  with bubble float, 82–83
Doll, use of, 65
Dolphin kicking, 124–25
Drills. See Swimming drills
Drowning statistics, 37

Eight-year-olds. See Advanced
    swimmers (five- to ten-
    year-olds)
Entering water with baby, 40
Eyes, opening under water, 88–
    89

Fearful children, 34
Fences, child-proof, 23
Five-year-olds. See Advanced
    swimmers (five- to ten-
    year-olds); Preschool
    children (three- to five-
    year-olds
Flippers, 26–27
Floatie armbands, 26
Floating
  on back, 90, 92

learning, 85–86
  preparation for, 43
  teaching, 43, 46–47, 50–52
Floats. See Bubble floats
Four-year-olds. See Preschool
    children (three- to five-
    year-olds)
Freestyle stroke, for competitive
    swimming, 133–34,
    136. See also Freestyle
    stroke, for five- to ten-
    year-olds
  arm movements, 134
  breathing for, 134, 136–37
  popularity of, 133
Freestyle stroke, for five- to ten-
    year-olds. See also Free-
    style stroke, for competi-
    tive swimming
  arm movements, 99–101
  breathing for, 101–4, 110
  coordination in, 108
  faults to watch for, 103–5,
    107–12
  head out of water in, 109
  kicking faults, 103–5
  teaching, 98–112
  ugly, 111–12

Games, in tub or shower, 20–21
Gates, 23
Gliding, 99
Goggles, 27

Hair, 25
  washing, 20–21
Holding breath, teaching, 42–
    43, 66, 89–90

Infants. See Babies, young

Jumping into water. See also
    Diving
  deep water, 113–16
  teaching, 92–93

Kicking
  on back, 90, 92
  backstroke, 126, 130–31
  with bubble floats, 77–78
  butterfly stroke, 122
  dolphin kicking, 124–25
  on edge of pool, 76
  freestyle, 103–5
Kicking boards, 23, 25, 80, 82
  "one-arm breathing" with,
    107
  swimming drills with, 112

Land drills, 112
Laziness, 108
Learning plateaus, 95–97
Learning rate, 16

Motivation, for competitive
    swimming, 118–20

Nine-year-olds. *See* Advanced
    swimmers (five- to ten-
    year-olds)

Olympic Games, 119
One-year-olds. *See* Babies,
    young; Toddlers to three
    years

Paddling, 57, 59
Parent, attitude of, 17, 19
Parent-and-child class, age for
    starting
Pool(s). *See* Swimming pool(s)
Pool safety, 22–24
  for babies, 47
  do's and don'ts, 23–24
  pool owners and, 22–23
  for preschool children, 54,
    59–60
  teaching, 22–23
Pool-cleaning equipment, 24
Practice, 137
Preparing child to swim, 16–17,
    19–20
Preschool children (three- to

five-year-olds), 69–97
  beginning classes, 72–74
  behavior of, 74
  class size, 69–70
  explaining to, 71–72, 82
  kicking boards for, 80, 82
  kicking on back, 90, 92
  learning plateaus of, 96
  making friends with, 74
  opening eyes under water,
    88–89
  paddling without bubble
    floats, 86, 88
  problems encountered in
    teaching, 77, 95–97
  sitting on edge of pool and
    kicking, 74, 76
  staying under water, 89–90
  swimming classes for, 69–71
  tantrums of, 77
  teaching bubble-blowing to,
    80–85
  teaching jumping and diving
    to, 92–93, 95
  working with bubble floats,
    76–80
Pushing, 99
Pushing off wall, 137

Rules. *See* Discipline

Safety around and in pool, 22–
    24
  for babies, 47
  do's and don'ts, 23–24
  pool owners and, 22–23
  for preschool children, 54,
    59–60
  teaching, 22–23
Schoolwork, and swimming, 120
Seven-year-olds. *See* Advanced
    swimmers (five- to ten-
    year-olds)
Showers, 19–20
Six-year-olds. *See* Advanced
    swimmers (five- to ten-
    year-olds)

Snorkels, 27
Splashing, 76
Staleness, 95–97
Staying under water, 89–90. *See also* Holding breath
Superbaby class, 38. *See also* Babies, young
Supervision, 23
Swimming, as way of life, 117–18, 120
Swimming aids, 24, 25–27. *See also specific aids, e.g.,* Bubble floats; Kicking boards
Swimming classes, 38–38
   observing, 39
   for three- to five-year-olds, 69–71
Swimming drills, for five- to ten-year-olds, 112
Swimming pool(s), 21–22
   backyard, recommendations for, 21–22
   depth of, 21, 54, 90, 108
   fence around, 23
   instructions near, 23
   shape of, 21–22
   familiarity of, 97
   ideal depth of, for preschool children, 54
Swimming suits, 24–25

Teaching baby at home, preliminary lessons, 40, 42–43
Teaching method, about, 15–16
Telephone, in pool area, 23
Three-year-olds. *See* Preschool children (three- to five-year-olds); Toddlers to three years
Toddlers to three years, 53–68
   duration of lessons, 65
   first water experiences, 54–56
   lessons, summarized, 68
   verbal instructions for, 56, 59–60, 65, 66–67
Toys, 19, 20
Two-year-olds. *See* Toddlers to three years

Vests, inflatable, 27

Walking age to three years. *See* Toddlers to three years
Walking in pairs (exercise), 123
Wall
   holding on to, 59–60
   pushing off, 137
Washing hair, 20–21
Water intake, signs of, 65
Weather, 70

ABOUT THE AUTHOR

EVA PAJOR BORY was born in Hungary. She describes her greatest thrill in swimming as swimming the 100 meter backstroke leg of the world-record-breaking medley team in 1955. She was a member of the Hungarian National Swimming Team at the 1956 Olympic Games in Melbourne, Australia.

After settling in Australia, she started teaching professionally in 1958 and pioneered methods of teaching how to swim that are now widely used throughout the world. She has worked with Forbes Carlile, the famous Australian Olympic coach, and with Don Talbot as well, coach of many Olympic champions. She has operated several swimming schools in Sydney, Australia, and one in Phoenix, Arizona. She is also a member of the board of directors of the National Swim School Association and the recipient of an Outstanding Teacher Award in 1990.